ESSENTIALS

of Capacity
Management

Essentials Series

The Essentials Series was created for busy business advisory and corporate professionals. The books in this series were designed so that these busy professionals can quickly acquire knowledge and skills in core business areas.

Each book provides need-to-have fundamentals for those professionals who must:

- Get up to speed quickly, because they have been promoted to a new position or have broadened their responsibility scope
- Manage a new functional area
- Brush up on new developments in their area of responsibility
- Add more value to their company or clients

Other books in this series include the following:

For more information on any of these titles, please visit www.wiley.com.

ESSENTIALS

of Capacity

Management

Reginald Tomas Yu-Lee

This publication is designed to provide accurate and authoritative information in regard to the subject matter covered. It is sold with the understanding that the publisher is not engaged in rendering legal, accounting, or other professional services. If legal advice or other expert assistance is required, the services of a competent professional should be sought.

ISBN 0-471-20746-2

Printed in the United States of America.

10 9 8 7 6 5 4 3 2 1

To my godfather, Charles Brantley, my late godmother, Jerry Brantley, and, as always, to my daughter, Erin

Preface

My editor, Sheck Cho, and I met over lunch one day at a restaurant in New York City in Spring, 2001. We talked a bit about the type of work that we were doing and what we were interested in doing. He brought up the *Essentials Series,* of which this book is a part. I thought that the idea of taking somewhat complicated subjects and explaining them in a way that is useable to the target audience of executives and others in upper-management positions was a very good one. As he mentioned the titles already in the series, I thought about some new ones that would be interesting and some that would be difficult. The prospective title that was both interesting and difficult happened to be the one before my readers now.

Capacity management is interesting because the concept is so pervasive, yet unnoticed. It is a nameless face that everyday walks among billions of people whose lives involve doing something productive. From the highest-level executives in organizations and governments to starving children in third world countries, it is our capacity and the effective utilization of capacity that allows us to build cars, govern people, and feed children.

Because the concept of capacity is as prevalent as it is, breaking it down into something relatively simple in a 200-plus page book is a difficult task. There are so many definitions of capacity, but few capture the true essence of what capacity is. Capacity is not just the bandwidth of a network or the amount of product that can be made on a machine. When looking at a company, capacity is comprised of practically all of the organization's resources that it uses to perform work. Buildings provide the space in which we work. People provide the ability to think, manage, and perform much of the work that is done in the firm. Equipment and information technology provide the tools that we use on a daily basis to create and use products, information, and data. The materials that a firm owns provide the capacity to make products. The money to which the firm has access provides the ability to invest in the ownership, creation, and management of its assets. These fundamental components, called *capacity entities,* are the base units of capacity and are combined to form operations. A machine may need materials and labor for it to perform its tasks, just as a payroll clerk needs a computer, stock for the checks, and a printer to create checks. Multiple operations are combined into the processes that the firm uses to create the work products necessary to function daily.

When considered from this perspective, capacity is one of the most important aspects of what employees within a firm must manage. And it must be managed at all levels. Upper-level executives may focus on the aggregate capacity within the firm. But even in the lower levels, decisions can be made that impact the efficient and effective utilization of capacity. A person choosing to do the wrong thing at the wrong time can wreak havoc on a process and its capacity. A highly capable person might be able to identify improvements that would lead to the creation of even more capacity without costing the organization time or money.

This book is an attempt to address the interesting and the difficult. The book will provide readers with a fundamental understanding of what capacity is, what it can do, how it is measured, its impact on the firm's financial dynamics, and how to use optimization techniques and ideas to improve and optimize capacity. Along the way, operations, processes, and an approach for managing capacity to ensure long-term effectiveness are discussed.

Chapter 1 begins with an introduction to capacity and capacity management by defining capacity and the pervasiveness of capacity within a company. It impacts the organization's cash flow, its capabilities and competencies, the products and services delivered, and brand image. Chapter 2 focuses on taking the capacity entities discussed in Chapter 1, focusing further on their characteristics, and describing how differing entities can come together to create operations. Chapter 3 discusses how to measure the types of capacity that can be created. Four fundamental measures are used and combined to provide ways to measure the amount of capacity that exists and how effectively it is being managed. Chapter 4 begins the discussion of processes by emphasizing the need to understand the purpose of a process. The purpose of the process includes issues such as for whom the output of the process is made, what they will do with it, where it is required, and so on. This helps managers maintain their focus when operating and managing processes. Chapter 5 involves taking this information and using it to determine how processes operate. Processes involve the interactions of operations and entities. The interactions create much of the complexities associated with managing processes. Managers must consider the aspects of a process, as described in Chapter 4, along with issues such as managing throughput and lead time. Chapter 6 introduces ways to understand capacity from a financial perspective.

The approach taken in this book is that cash flow is king. So, this chapter talks about the financial impact of capacity from the perspective of both the impact that it has on the bottom line and how it impacts the bottom line. Chapter 7 introduces the concept of optimization. Optimizing process capacity involves identifying the objective, whether operational or financial, and Chapter 7 discusses the activities and requirements necessary to optimize processes. Also, in the absence of being able to perform the true optimization of a process, the chapter talks about what we learn from the optimization of a process to improve its operations. Finally, Chapter 8 introduces a closed-loop approach for managing capacity to ensure that it is aligned as closely with the demands being placed on it as is organizationally possible.

I hope that the book meets your expectations. The topic is one that cannot be covered in its entirety here, and so this book will likely create many conversations within organizations. If there are any questions or comments, I would love to hear from you at dr_reginald@att.net.

Acknowledgments

This book was written during one of the most difficult times in my life. After agreeing to write the book, my godmother died unexpectedly, the tragic events of September 11th occurred, and I went from being a bachelor to being a single father to my 10-year-old daughter. During this time, I lived off of the support a few key people. My mother, Fred, practically managed my life for a period of two months or so. I will never, ever be able to thank her enough for her support. My daughter, Erin, who let me sleep when I needed to sleep, woke me up when I needed to get up, or pulled out our favorite video game, *Mario Kart,* when she needed to get beaten by dad, played a key role. She is the best daughter that I could ever imagine having. My sister, Wynnette, provided significant support when it came to allowing my daughter to stay with her during difficult times. My brother, Marc, his wife, Adriana, and my nephews, Marcus and Michael (Santana), are, as always, wonderful for the support that they provide.

The Hernandi (we chose this over "the Hernandezes") are a great group to be around: Briana and Christina were among Erin's first friends, and together there were lots of laughs, fun, and relaxing times, except when playing *Pictionary.* Janet also pitched in to do some typing at a key moment. Thank you so much, Janet, for everything. My very good friend Valerie Wahl (a.k.a. Athena) was a strong supporter from the beginning. The woman is brilliant and is a great source of inspiration, ideas, laughs, and grammar corrections. My boss, Steve Hoffman, provided the moral support to get through this and has been a great source of inspiration. Thanks. Martin J. often kept me fed when there was no time to cook. If you ever want macadamia nut cookies, go to Martin J. Leanne Montgomery did a great job bailing me out of a few situations with her 80-words-per-minute skills and great attitude. The guys at "The Tavern," Steve, Dave, Ramon, Church, Richard, and Dom, always allowed me to work in peace when working at home was too quiet. Christy, thanks for always having the right words (such as *quaternary*). Rob DeBoer from "Four80East" made sure that I had their incredible music to listen to during the long nights of typing and writing. Thanks, Rob. Check out their music—it's great. I also listened to the music of a very cool group of musicians, Hiroshima, to help relax. June, thanks again for the great music, and I am sorry I missed you guys in L.A. My editor, Sheck Cho, will probably not believe another deadline promise that I make to him—ever. Without his support, flexibility, and faith in me, none of this would be a reality. As always, Pepé was there to provide his inspiring support when I was at a loss for words or ideas. Finally, thanks to all of my friends who supported me as I went underground to write this book. The e-mails, the phone calls, the cards—everything was great. Thank you for your support.

Contents

CHAPTER 1

Capacity Management

 After reading this chapter you will be able to:

- Define capacity and capacity competence
- Understand how capacity impacts an organization's cash flow
- Develop an appreciation for how capacity impacts organizational capabilities
- Understand, fundamentally, how capacity management impacts brand image
- Articulate a basic approach for managing capacity

Defining Capacity Management

What Is Capacity?

Managing organizational capacity is one of the most underestimated, and, therefore, poorly performed, activities in organizational management. The capacity of an organization represents its ability to perform work. This capacity manifests itself in many ways including space, labor, equipment, technology, and materials. We often underestimate the importance of capacity management because we fail to understand it in its entirety. Capacity management involves managing the amount of what the organization has and uses to perform work. An organization will, therefore, use its space as offices, production facilities, warehouses, and in other ways to house work that will be done. Its labor or people perform the tasks associated with completing work. Its equipment often performs tasks that are either not humanly possible or that are much more efficient if automated. Robots, for example, can operate in very hazardous environments in which humans would not consider working. Huge stamping machines can create precise replications of automobile fenders that humans would not be able to create, given time and precision constraints. Its computer technology facilitates analysis and decision making that requires the information that it creates or collects. Computer technology is also used as a medium to perform repetitive data-oriented transactions. Finally, an organization uses its purchased material capacity to meet anticipated demand from its customers.

We do not often look at a process, such as product development, as the capacity of scientists, engineers, and technicians to develop new products. We do not look at sales as the capacity of our sales people and their support personnel to sell new products, or accounting as the capacity of accountants, their support staff, and their systems to report costs, pay bills, and collect on monies due. This, however, is exactly what capacity is. Organizations pay for people, space, information technology, equipment, and materials. They buy the capacity to do work. There are only so many people working in a facility. A factory is only so big and can therefore handle a limited amount of equipment and labor. Information systems are only capable of performing so many transactions per unit of time. Companies buy and make investments in what ultimately becomes its capacity to operate—to do some type of work.

Often, various types of capacity are combined to perform work. For example, people, equipment, and materials come together to make products. People, space, and technology can come together to provide services. The total capacity of an organization is determined by how it combines and utilizes the capacity it has purchased to perform work. However, the relationship between individual units of capacity and the total capacity is not perfectly correlated. Some organizations are able to combine their capacity more effectively than can other organizations. They can get more work done with the same amount of capacity. To achieve desirable financial performance, it is important for organizations to be able to manage this capacity effectively. Understanding future demand and adjusting capacity to meet this demand effectively is a sine qua non for ensuring that the sales and costs figures are in line to achieve the anticipated financial performance.

Companies must, therefore, have a complete understanding of what their capacity is capable of creating and delivering. This capability, which will be referred to as the organization's *capacity competence,* can be tied to the utilization, efficiency, productivity, planning, and management of its capacity as well as to its ability to predict future demand.

Capacity Competence

Capacity competence reflects what an organization can achieve from its capacity. Consider two similar organizations in similar industries. Assume, for the sake of illustration, that the organizations are of similar size, similar complexity, have similar processes, and produce similar products. One organization has an accounting department of 50 people, whereas the second organization has a staff of 100. One can assume that the capacity of the former organization is more competent than the capacity of the latter. Why? Because it can accomplish more with its capacity. The capacity is more competent in terms of getting its job done. It must be made clear that competence in this case may not reflect the capabilities of the capacity that makes up the ability to perform the work. The organization with 100 people may have brilliant accountants with exceptional tools. Instead, competence represents how much work can get done, given the environment in which work is being performed. The rules, regulations, and processes can often impact an organization's ability to perform work and, therefore, its capacity competence.

Why is this? Capacity competence is comprised of three components:

- Physical-capacity competence
- Operational/process-related competence
- Management-influenced competence

All three will ultimately impact competence either positively or negatively.

Physical-capacity competence comes from combining various types of physical capacity to perform work. A machine with a person and materials can only perform so much work in a given period of time. A computer and its network can only handle so many transactions per unit of time. A building can only handle so many people or so much equipment or both. Each of these combinations has physical limitations, both as individual capacity components and as combinations. This natural limit provides a constraint inside of which managers must operate.

Capacity competence is not only determined by the physical ability of the capacity to perform designated functions. The operation or process itself can have an impact on capacity competence. For example, a poorly designed process can limit what a man–machine combination can perform. Although the man and the machine are both available for the same eight hours in a shift, one combination may have streamlined tasks or functions. Another combination may have activities that do not add value to the final product, and may also add to the length of time required to complete the task. The first combination can be considered to be more competent, because it can get more value-added work accomplished in an equal amount of time.

Finally, there is a management component to capacity competence. Improperly managing, scheduling, or operating processes or operations can have a significant impact on capacity competence. As discussed in Chapters 5 and 7, poor management decisions and competence-limiting rules can lead to suboptimal performance, regardless of how effectively the process has been defined or the competence of the people.

Capacity competence is an idea that will be revisited many times throughout this book. It is stated here as elsewhere that capacity competence itself should not be considered as the key criterion or ultimate measure upon which capacity-related decisions are made. As will be seen in the optimization discussions in Chapter 7, considering capacity from a macro level helps organizations make decisions that are more effective in terms of achieving desirable operational and financial results.

Why Is Capacity Management Important?

In the past, capacity was often incompletely defined. When managing operations, for example, the capacity of an operation was determined by its time standards, and operational standards, and the time that the operation was available. For example, a machine that can process 20 parts per hour during an 8-hour shift is theoretically capable of producing 160 units

TIPS & TECHNIQUES

When you think about the capacity competence of your organization, what is the immediate reaction? With the most important strategic capacity, are you mostly behind, on par, or ahead of your competitors? Why?

over the shift. Capacity was also applied to information systems and networks to represent the number of transactions or users that can be supported. Systems had the capacity to support only so many concurrent users or so many transactions per unit time and were incapable of handling more.

However, an organization's capacity is much larger than that considered by these definitions. Labor capacity is often required to operate, schedule, and maintain the equipment. It is also required to engage in activities such as selling the work that will be processed by the machines, purchasing the materials that will be used to support the machines, and practically all of the other functions associated with operating the organization. Building capacity is often necessary to house the labor capacity, equipment capacity, information technology capacity, and material capacity. Organizations buy materials in anticipation of demand. These materials provide the organization with the capacity to produce its products quickly. When capacity is properly categorized, it can quickly become one of the most important aspects of managing an organization for the following reasons:

- Capacity represents a significant majority of a firm's costs.
- Capacity represents a large amount of a firm's assets.
- Improperly managing capacity limits the firm's cash flow.
- Managing capacity impacts overall ability to operate and perform.

- Capacity and capacity competence impact the organization's brand and brand image.

Capacity Is a Significant Component of a Firm's Costs

When you think of capacity as space, labor, equipment, information technology, and materials, you can begin to see that capacity makes up a significant portion of an organization's costs. Consider major categories on the income statement and statement of cash flows, such as cost of goods sold (COGS), sales, general and administrative costs (SGA), and property, plant, and equipment costs. Capacity is a significant contributor to the value of each. The next few sections will discuss why in detail.

Cost of Goods Sold

The COGS involves determining the costs of the products sold on the market. Clearly, the inventory used to make the products becomes a large component of this cost. Another, and often larger, cost, however, is the labor that is involved in making the products. Direct and indirect labor at the plant level are often allocated to the cost of a product being made. So, the financial worth of inventory increases as labor performs its tasks to transform the materials from their raw form to something that is usable and ultimately salable. A piece of in-process inventory that has not completed the assigned production steps is financially worth more than the material in its raw state, even though the market value of the in-process inventory is really less.[1] It is from here that the concept of adding value to inventory comes. As labor processes the material, its financial value from an accounting perspective increases. The COGS, therefore, will include the costs that are involved with transforming raw materials into salable products. These costs are often significant with respect to their impact on the bottom line.

Sales, General, and Administrative

The SGA cost category is somewhat of a catchall, in that many expense types can be placed in this category. It basically represents the organization's operating expenses. Because of this, there is a significant amount of costs or expenses in both volume and magnitude that are tied to this value. This includes various types of capacity expenses. Many of the labor capacity costs, for example, that are not captured in the COGS are captured within SGA. Even if one only considers labor costs, the value can be pretty substantial. However, other types of capacity items, depending on how an organization categorizes its capacity types, make up SGA, leading to a value that cannot be ignored by management.

Property, Plant, and Equipment

Financially, the value used for property, plant, and equipment (PP&E) represents the investments that an organization plans to use over a fairly long period of time. This will include the various buildings that the organization will buy for office, manufacturing, and storage purposes, as well as much of the equipment that is used in this space. Therefore, this will often include a manufacturing plant, the equipment that is used for the manufacturing processes, and the IT systems used to manage and control this equipment. Space, equipment, and IT can, in many cases, constitute a significant portion of the value of an organization's PP&E line item.

Capacity Represents a Large Amount of a Firm's Assets

An asset represents that to which an organization has access. This will include certain financial categories, such as an organization's cash, its assets used for operations such as machinery, and other, often important assets, such as intellectual capacity. There is also a very-difficult-to-measure, but nevertheless important, asset—its people.

When looking at an organization's balance sheet, one will observe the impact of capacity. Inventory that has not been converted to COGS is represented on the balance sheet. This includes raw materials, in-process materials, and finished goods. Unsold-finished-goods inventory represents the capacity of an organization to deliver products from its inventory. If, for example, the organization has ten widgets, it theoretically has the capacity to meet an order for ten widgets. It can also meet any demand that it may incur for any value below ten widgets. If an order comes in for any value above ten widgets, the organization will not have the capacity to deliver. Property, plant, and equipment is a value that is actually represented on the balance sheet as a component of a firm's assets.

Not necessarily represented explicitly on the balance sheet as assets are the knowledge and experiences of an organization's people. The organization has access to information and skills that have been developed over time that allow a machine operator to create new and innovative ways to manufacture or design a component part. It allows the inventory manager to determine whether sales forecasts are accurate, so that the organization does not overproduce. It allows an engineer to design using new materials or to use existing materials in different ways.

This knowledge is extremely important to an organization's ability to do its work. It can actually measurably increase an organization's capacity to produce. This is represented by ideas such as the learning or experience curve, which suggests that the more often a person performs a task, the better he or she will become at performing the task. This, over time, has a significant impact on an organization's ability to manage capacity at the lowest levels required to meet expected demand.

So, both traditional measurable assets and knowledge assets can have an impact on the capacity of an organization. Clearly, the more traditional assets are easier to measure from both a physical and a financial perspective. However, this does not make knowledge, as an asset, any less important. Knowledge, in fact, will be one of the most critical aspects necessary to manage the organization's capacity effectively.

Capacity Impacts a Firm's Ability to Manage Cash Flow

Cash flow is highly impacted by an organization's capacity. At the highest levels, cash flow is impacted by an organization's ability to cut costs, increase revenues, and improve its working capital by reducing its magnitude. As discussed previously, the costs that an organization incurs have capacity components to them, comprised of the labor, land, machines, computers, and materials. Clearly, the cost impact on working capital is substantial. However, managers must also manage revenue-lift and working capital to ensure that the organization is in a desirable position with regard to its cash flow.

Revenue

The market demand for an organiztion's products and its capacity to meet this demand largely determine the organization's revenue. When the demand exceeds the capacity, increasing the capacity and acting on this increase will increase the revenues of the firm. This is because the capacity constrains the organization's ability to meet demand. If the organization were able to make more of its products, the market would buy them. If the market constrains revenue growth, the organization's capacity may be too high for that particular period and managers may need to consider whether the organization has the proper capacity levels to meet current and future demand.

To get the most from its capacity from a revenue perspective, one must clearly understand what demands will be placed on the organization, what its capacity is, and the trends that might impact each of them.

Developing Knowledge as an Asset

In today's working environment, managing knowledge is ever more important. As information technology becomes more prevalent, we can see two major trends. First, information systems are increasingly able to make not only routine decisions but more advanced decisions, as well. This limits the need for humans to make such decisions. The complexity of the decisions that humans will have to make over time will increase. Second, computers make knowledge information storage and knowledge sharing much easier today than ever before.

Since knowledge and the resulting competencc is an organization's only appreciable asset,[a] organizations must have strategies in place to manage both. From a competence-building perspective, Ulrich suggests that successful companies will have to embark on a strategy that allows them to:

- Gain access to the best and the brightest through hiring, developing, or using consulting services
- Develop a strategy to keep the competent and committed workers
- Rid themselves of workers who cannot change or grow with the organization

The organization must also have an infrastructure to support its workers. In addition to recognizing the humanistic needs of the workers, this would include training and providing access to data and information through knowledge management. The knowledge management approaches that exist are either a codification strategy, where knowledge is captured for reuse, or a personalization strategy, where individuals share their knowledge with each other with conversations facilitated by information technology.[b] The firm must select its approach to knowledge management based on the needs

(CONTINUED)

IN THE REAL WORLD (CONTINUED)

dictated by the firm's overall strategy and its strategy for developing and maintaining the competence of its employees.

[a] Dave Ulrich, "Intellectual Capital = Competence × Commitment," *Sloan Management Review* 39, 2 (Winter 1998).

[b] Morton T. Hansen, Nitin Nohria, and Thomas Tierney, "What's Your Strategy for Managing Knowledge?" *Harvard Business Review* 77, 2 (March-April 1999).

If there were an upward trend in market demand, the organization should understand the implications of this trend on its ability to deliver and the financial results. If, for example, it does not have enough capacity, it might consider increasing its capacity at a rate in accordance with its strategy and growth capabilities and investor expectations. If, however, there exists too much capacity, the organization might consider maintaining its current capacity or consider reducing it at a slower rate than it may have previously considered.

When considered independently of cost management and working-capital management, the idea is to align capacity with demand. Many organizations have looked at capacity management from a demand perspective only. Doing so might lead to other issues that will ultimately suboptimize profits and cash flows by creating negative working capital positions. These undesirable positions for both cost and working capital may dominate, negatively, the positive influence created by focusing on demand. Examples are carrying too much inventory for the demand that might lead to less than desirable investment returns for the capital tied up in the inventory. Another might be increasing costs at a rate that is not offset by revenue growth, as was seen by many consultancies attempting to address an anticipated boom in internet consulting services.

Therefore, as an organization ultimately seeks to optimize its cash flow and profitability positions, it must not only think of focusing on revenue-increasing options. Revenues must be balanced with information about what the market demand will be and what organizational structure and capacity will be necessary to effectively meet the market needs.

Working Capital

The working capital of a firm represents its capital tied up in inventory, accounts payable (what the firm owes to others), and accounts receivable (what others owe to the firm). Longer cycles of accounts payable (discussed in more detail in Chapter 6) suggest that the organization keeps its money for longer periods. This may or may not be a bad thing, depending on its impact on the entity to which the money is owed and whether there are penalties for late payment. With accounts receivable, the firm is in the position of trying to collect its money. Clearly, from a cash flow perspective, this cycle should be as short as possible. With inventory, the concerns involve the amount of time that a firm's money is tied up in inventory that is not generating revenues for the firm and the amount of money that the firm has tied up in its inventory.

Accounts Receivables

Accounts receivable, or receivables, represent the amount of money that other organizations owe a company. So, upon buying a product or a service, a firm is invoiced and has a payment period that, upon conclusion, requires payment. Although this period is often designed to be 30 to 45 days, it is often much longer. Issues, such as improperly created invoices, incomplete invoices, invoices that are not sent out in a timely fashion, a lack of focus on collections, and others, can lengthen the cycle. People and IT capacity, and their combined capacity competence, when applied to this process will impact the length of the cycle. The ability for the process to deliver invoices correctly and on time, the ability to perform and accept electronic payments, and the ability to follow up on late payments are all able to improve the receivables position of a firm. As discussed in Chapters 6 and 7, effective capacity management can help lead to optimized financial performance.

Inventory

Inventory is a critical area to manage from a working-capital perspective. As a firm forecasts what its future demand will be, it often builds inventory capacity to meet the demand in a quick and efficient manner. As with all other types of capacity, inventory costs money. It is an investment in materials that will hopefully pay off. The payoff does not necessarily occur because inventory purchases and creation are often truly independent of actual demand. For many organizations, purchases are based on forecasted demand, which, by definition, is an estimate of what the actual demand might be. This will lead to situations in which too much, or not enough, inventory is purchased or created. When too much inventory is created, organizations end up using their cash and capacity to create inventory for which there is no demand.

From a working-capital perspective, this is not positive for the organization. First, the organization must pay for the inventory. This cash, which could be used for other investments, is now tied to the inventory and the capacity that it creates. The cash is tied up from the time that the inventory is paid for until the time that it is sold as a product or, in another state, including its raw form. This process can take weeks but often takes many months to occur. Second, the inventory can become obsolete, meaning that the firm will receive much less than the sales price anticipated. Having too much inventory is similar to having too many people. Again, if the demand is for 5 units and the organization has 10 units in inventory, the extra 5 units will go unused, just as if the needed capacity for a services company is five people yet it has ten available. In both cases, money is directed toward capacity that is not making money for the firm.

Capacity Impacts Overall Ability to Operate and Perform

In general, capacity directly impacts how a firm operates and what it can accomplish. Simply, the work that an organization does is based on how it can, and how it chooses to, use its capacity. The organization combines its space, people, machines, IT, and materials to perform the necessary tasks to allow it to compete in its respective market. The capacity determines how much can get done in a period of time. More capacity will often have a higher number of activities that can be performed with it than less capacity. More capacity competence allows the organization to do more with the same capacity. In both cases, the organization must focus on performing the requisite tasks as efficiently and effectively as possible.

It becomes clear, therefore, that it is the organization's capacity and capacity competence that impacts its ability to perform activities such as:

- Development of new products and services
- Production
- Service delivery
- Response to changes in demand
- Everyday operations

Developing New Products and Services

New product and service development brings together many capabilities and competencies of the organization's capacity. Its scientific capacity impacts the speed and capability to create, develop, and deliver its theoretical and applied research. Its engineering and manufacturing capacities work together to develop products that are both perceived to be desired by the market and are efficient to make. Marketing capacity determines both the rate at which the market need can be validated and information about the products or services disseminated.

Production

Manufacturing capacity determines the rate at which products can be introduced to the market and manufactured at a desired output rate. This involves the ability of production to develop the systems that are going to be used to make the products, test the systems, introduce the new products, and bring them up to regular manufacturing levels. This also involves the ability to identify bugs and inefficiencies in processes that may lead to less-than-optimal performance and quality and to repair them to minimize their impact. Capacity involves the ability of the organization to manage the inventory, pick, pack, and ship products, and invoice customers. All in all, practically all of an organization's production capability is tied to its capacity.

Service Delivery

Although perhaps not immediately obvious, service delivery is likely to be tied more to its capacity than is a manufacturing firm. It is probably not as obvious because of how capacity is more traditionally defined. Consider these examples.

Services Firm

The ability of a services firm to deliver its services is tied directly to the capacity that it has. There is a physical limit to the amount of consulting that consultants or lawyers can provide for their firms for example. Although there is the opportunity to provide automated consulting and law-based services via software and web-based solutions, nothing is available with current technological capabilities that can replace the knowledge gained and disseminated by having a consultant interview workers and make experience-based recommendations or a lawyer fighting a case in court. Many, however, would likely welcome the technology! There are a limited number of lawyers who can fight a case. There are a limited number of researchers who can find information. There are a limited number of strategists in a firm who can provide strategy consulting to its clients. The same goes for the IT capacity. There are physical limits to what the IT systems are capable of performing. Even a center providing supercomputing services is limited by the ability of the lines that feed the supercomputing center, and demand placed on the center, and the capabilities of the processors themselves. Services, therefore, are limited directly by the capacity that the firm has and its competence to deliver.

Retail Store

A retail environment has some of the same constraints as a services firm, whether the firm is a physical location or web-based. For these firms, traditionally, people constitute the capacity for labor-centric activities. Physical locations create capacity for both serving and storing merchandise and the inventory of products being sold. Another component to consider for many companies in the web-space is the more recent outsourcing environments that are being set up. Some companies may advertise, and even sell goods, for another organization from their web site. In cases like these, the ability to buy inventory or access to inventory creates another variable to consider from demand and service perspectives and creates another capacity constraint to consider. The inventory might not be available immediately from the third party, for example, which would limit the ability to serve customers. Also, future access to inventory might be limited, which might, in turn, limit the firm's ability to increase its capacity in the future.

Responding to Changes in Demand

To achieve the desired financial performance, organizations must be able to align their capacity with demand. In terms of managing the organization's finances, understanding and managing capacity and capacity competence are critical in helping an organization meet its objectives. Often, organizations are faced with either changes in demand-volume or changes in demand-type. In both cases, the organization is required to make decisions regarding whether to increase capacity, reduce capacity, or change the tasks performed by the capacity. How the firm responds can be of critical importance. Effectively responding to changes in demand will help maintain or increase customer satisfaction, while also helping to ensure that the desired level of financial performance is maintained.

Understanding Changes in Demand-Volume

One of the most difficult tasks of an organization is trying to figure out the size of the organization necessary for the anticipated demand. First, it must anticipate the demand. Forecasting is a very difficult task to do correctly, except in cases where one can pretty much assume that demand will not change regularly. This would include products or services where the demand rarely changes, or changes minimally from year to year, regardless of seasonality or economic issues. For organizations in such an environment, there might be a slight upward or downward trend, but the patterns and magnitudes do not change unpredictably. Capacity is easier to align with demand in such situations. For other firms, however, it becomes a task that most perform poorly.

Without knowing future demand, organizations will not get their capacity models correct. This should just be an accepted fact. The issue, then, is how organizations can manage the difference between the actual demand and the model created with the anticipated demand, so that financial and customer satisfaction issues are minimized. Flexibility in capacity and capacity competence helps organizations deal with volume fluctuations. For example, a lean and highly capable organization will be more *elastic* in terms of meeting its demand. "Elastic" in this sense means that it has a wide range of capability in terms of being able to perform its work. So, a highly capable organization might have a minimum capacity of 5 units but can handle up to 10 units if necessary. Fluctuations between 5 and 10 in this case will have a minimum impact on the capacity and, therefore, the cost component of the organization's financials. However, the same organization, if less elastic, may have a maximum capacity of 7 units. Fluctuations of up to 10 will either cause the organization to need to increase its capacity at some cost to meet the excess demand or to forego the revenues attainable at demand levels above 7.

Organizations must, therefore, understand and effectively measure their capacity and capacity competence and constantly strive to improve their management of both, so that they can operate at desirable financial and customer service levels.

Understanding Changes in Demand-Type

Changes in demand-type may or may not impact direct capacity per se. For example, assume that a firm makes two products: A and B. The replacement for B, which we will call C, will be phased in over a period of time, as B is phased out. If B and C have similar production requirements, it is possible in this simple case that overall capacity might not change. However, the capacity competence must be such that these shifts are, in fact, possible. The objective is to maintain output for A while producing B and C at desirable levels. With capacity competence comes the ability to quickly shift to the new product, thereby minimizing the financial and service aspects of making the changes. Without the required competencies, organizations might find themselves tied to product B, though there might be declining demand for the product, or unable to make enough of A, as resources are shifted to manage the transition from B to C. This, clearly, will minimize their ability to maintain or improve its financial performance.

Capacity Influences Everyday Operations

The ability to perform everyday tasks is also tied to an organization's capacity. From human resources to providing IT services to the executives, who set the direction of the firm, the capacity and the competence of that capacity will dictate what and how much can be done. One HR specialist usually cannot accomplish as much as three with the same competencies. Therefore, organizations with one specialist and significant HR requirements may find that some tasks are left undone as a result. Additionally, an HR organization with one capable person and the right IT capacity and capability might be able to perform more than ten HR specialists who are less competent. The same goes for sales, marketing, procurement, and other functional areas required to operate the firm.

Capacity Impacts the Brand and Brand Image

Customer service is a topic area that has been mentioned a number of times already in the book. For the sake of simplicity in this chapter, customer service reflects the ability of a firm to provide the right products when the market demands them. When visiting a retail store, for instance, those with the desired products in hand will have higher customer service levels.

Higher customer service levels will allow the organization to serve the customer, thereby increasing its revenues and its image in the market.[2] Organizations that fail to serve the customer will find themselves with dissatisfied customers or future customers. It may also find itself with a negatively impacted brand.[3] Grocery stores with low quality or low quantities of produce fit this bill. Customers looking to buy produce will walk away unsatisfied, which leaves the organization without selling its product. If this continues, the stores will find that customers will look elsewhere for their produce. This will help create and support a negative brand image of being a grocery store with poor produce.

The capacity of an organization can have a significant impact on its brand image. From a space perspective, how the space is designed and how the customers will interact with the space may help enhance brand. From a labor perspective, having people who can provide information, products, and other services in a proper and timely manner may enhance brand. From an equipment perspective, manufacturing and delivering quality products on time can create a positive brand image. From an IT perspective, having information that is available for customers or that can be used to serve customers better will have a positive impact. Finally, the right material capacity helps ensure that the right products can be made available to customers.

It should be apparent from these points that capacity can have a sometimes significant impact on how others view a firm in its market. Organizations will want to manage their capacity to ensure not only the desired financial results but also the desired brand image. As Coca-Cola and Nike can attest, strong positive brands can ultimately have a positive impact on the firm's financials.

Underestimating the Role of Capacity Management

Historically, organizations have not effectively managed their total capacity, quite simply because traditional definitions of capacity limit the understanding of that which constitutes capacity. Definitions that only focus on IT capacity, for instance, fail to acknowledge space, labor, equipment, and materials. Definitions that focus on equipment fail to acknowledge materials, labor, IT, and space. What is also missing, by definition, is the capability created when combining various types of capacity. As discussed in Chapter 2 and used beyond, space, labor, equipment, IT, and materials are only primary components of capacity or entities. When combined, two primary components can create secondary components of capacity or operations. For example, a machine working on a piece of equipment creates capacity to perform a task or a set of tasks for a particular operation. Multiple secondary levels can create tertiary capacity components or processes. Multiple worker-equipment combinations, along with materials, may create the capacity to physically produce some sort of an item. Finally, tertiary levels can be combined to create quaternary components of capacity, which involve the much more complex interaction of processes that create even more capabilities for the entire organization.

Without a complete understanding of what capacity exists at primary, secondary, tertiary, and quaternary levels, it becomes very difficult, if not impossible, to really understand the overall capacity, and, therefore, capabilities, of the organization. Without effectively managing the organization, the financial performance will most likely be less than desirable. Many organizations are still at the point where they have not acknowledged some of the primary capacity components, so a robust definition of secondary components is not something that can be accomplished, leading organizations to make decisions on often incomplete data and information about the capacity and capabilities of the organization. This is a major issue when one considers the points made earlier about the impact of capacity on the income statement, cash flow statements, and balance sheet. The numbers and the impact of positively or negatively managing capacity are immense. Therefore, managers everywhere should take a different look at capacity and how it impacts their jobs.

What Will Make Capacity Management More Prominent?

Once managers begin to understand the relative impact of capacity on an organization, the word should spread fairly quickly. However, the implementation of capacity management essentials will be limited if enough information about capacity does not exist. Therefore, one key criterion that has been established for this book is to identify and measure capacity at all levels from entity through process. Another criterion that must be set is to provide enough information and impetus to figure out new and better ways to define, measure, and manage capacity. This should be by no means the final book on capacity management. Rather, it should spawn thought about new and more effective ways to bring a firm's resources together to create new capabilities and competencies. It is from this and similar capabilities that leaders within their respective markets will emerge.

Is Not Capacity Difficult to Manage?

Understanding capacity and its measures is not enough to get the most out of the capacity. Capacity in its primary form can be complicated to understand. Terms, such as efficiency and utilization for primary components of capacity, will keep those who measure and manage capacity on their toes. Additionally, all of the data and information in the world might not have an impact if they fail to meet the needs of those making the decisions about how the capacity should be used.

TIPS & TECHNIQUES

1. Think about your organization's understanding of capacity. Is it sufficient, given the range of influence that capacity has?

2. Think about the decisions that are made. Would they change? How would decision-makers operate differently with this information?

3. What role can you play to ensure that your organization is well prepared to manage its capacity?

Simply, to get the most from a firm's capacity, it needs to focus on:

- Setting organizational objectives and priorities
- Forecasting the demand for capacity
- Planning and responding to expected demand
- Closing the loop

Setting Organizational Objectives and Priorities

There should be no ambiguity about what the organization's strategy and objectives should be at all levels of the organization. This strategy is what should be used by the organization to create the context of how the capacity will be managed. What are the revenue and cost targets? What are the inventory levels? What are the customer service and customer satisfaction levels? This type of information is what should be used, so that the capacity plan and capacity management objectives can be defined to meet that required by the organization's goals and objectives.

Forecasting the Demand for Capacity

Once the goals and objectives for operations and capacity are in place, the organization will then be required to effectively forecast the demand. There are a number of ways to forecast demand, ranging from taking the actual numbers from the previous year to using sophisticated techniques and tools to attempt to find the most accurate forecast available. Whatever technique is used, two issues must be kept in mind. First, some attempt at forecasting should be made. Second, the accuracy of the forecast must be constantly determined, because if the organization is planning its capacity to incorrect data and information, the overall performance will be less than desired.

Planning and Responding to Expected Demand

Once the demand is understood, the organization must make its adjustments to capacity to meet the needs of both the demand and the

24

organizational objectives. This means being flexible enough to increase capacity or reduce capacity with minimal increases or decreases to that which creates capacity, such as the number of people or the number of machines. It also means being flexible to the extent that the organizations can adjust to changes in the nature of the demand. If products are being phased out for new products, the organization must have the competence to handle the old products, the new products, and the challenges created by the transition. The changes must occur quickly, so that the organization does not miss out on revenue enhancement or cost reduction opportunities, as will be discussed in Chapter 6.

Closing the Loop

Finally, the organization must close the loop. This means taking information, such as the demand deviations that existed for the period (actual demand versus forecasted demand), the responsiveness of the organizations to changes in data, and the impact on financial and customer service aspects of operations to find ways to improve. An organization will never be perfect at forecasting and adjusting to the forecast, so, as long as it is not perfect, there is room to improve.

Summary

Capacity influences all aspects of a firm's operations and finances. From its ability to design, develop, produce, and deliver products and services to practically dominating the financial statements, organizations may find themselves ill-prepared with respect to understanding how to properly manage their capacity. Managers should begin to think about capacity in terms of its basic forms: entities, operations, and processes. With a common understanding of just how expansive the reach of capacity management is, managers can begin to make the decisions that elevate the importance of capacity management and can begin to improve their strategy and operations.

Endnotes

[1] Material in its raw state should have higher market value because other organizations can still process it with its unique processes. However, in-process materials are likely to have states specific to the unique production steps of a particular company, leading to a reduction in its market value.

[2] There is a cost of maintaining higher customer service levels. For example, higher inventory levels are often required to ensure high customer service levels. So, although the revenues may increase, the costs may, too. This concept is discussed in Chapter 3.

[3] Some organizations may choose to incorporate a somewhat exclusive strategy in which its products and services are only available to a few customers. Such a strategy may increase the brand image of the product, but is limited to products for which there are few or no substitutions.

CHAPTER 2

Defining Entity Capacity and Operation Capacity

After reading this chapter you will be able to:

- Define the various capacity types and their characteristics
- Understand how capacity entities can be combined to create increased entity capacity
- Understand how capacity entities can be combined to create operations

Introduction

Before proceeding into measuring and managing capacity, it will be important to define the various types of capacity in some detail. The purpose is to create an operating definition of capacity and to ensure that all of the readers look at capacity the same way for the rest of this book. This is especially important in the next chapter, as the ways to measure capacity are introduced. In the past, capacity was defined in a much more limited fashion than it is in this book. In manufacturing, for example, capacity often focused on production-related operations. Techniques for utilization and efficiency were created to help engineers and planners understand how much time capacity existed for each operation. This limited view of capacity became very apparent when Eliyahu Goldratt introduced a practical understanding of process optimization with his theory of constraints (TOC).[1] It was arguably at this moment that a more thorough understanding of processes and the interaction of operations within the process generally arose.

This understanding must be expanded to the organization at large. The theory of constraints is a very good primer that can be used to help organizations understand how to manage and use their capacity. The capacity components can be defined independently, however; the capability of the organization will be determined by how the components interact to perform work and how the components, their interactions, and their output are managed.

This chapter will focus on initially identifying the capacity components. It is important to do so because these components, called *capacity entities* or *entities*, are the basic elements for organizational operations. The capacity entities are space, labor, equipment, information technology (IT), and material. Using these entities as building blocks, operational capabilities will be defined by combining the entities. These operational capabilities will include, for example, space-labor interactions, labor-equipment interactions, labor-IT interactions, and material-equipment interactions. Chapter 3 will focus on measuring operations that are defined in this chapter.

Chapter 4, devoted to processes, will then shift to a secondary level of interaction between capacity components. Labor-machine operating combinations, for example, may be assembled to create processes. The processes are measured and managed differently than the operational level combinations because of the issues related to their interactions and the need to focus on the output of the system that they create.

For the concepts introduced in this book to be useful, it is important for the readers to open up to a different definition of what types of capacity exist. It will then be necessary to apply, somewhat differently, existing techniques and measures to begin understanding how to manage the capacity combinations that exist within your firm. As discussed in Chapter 1, there are five different types of capacity: space, labor, equipment, IT, and material. The rest of the section will focus on defining each component for use throughout the book. A set of commonly used terms will be defined for use throughout this and other chapters. These are:

- Capacity entity or entity
- Operational capacity or operation
- Process capacity or process
- Organizational capacity or organization

Entities are the basic components of capacity. Space, labor, equipment, IT, and materials are all entities. Operations reflect the combination of entities. Process capacity is the combination of operations for the purpose of creating a specific usable product, item, or service. Finally, organizational capacity involves the creation of organizational capabilities by combining processes.

Entity Capacity

Entities are the lowest-level capacity components that an organization needs to manage. Breaking them down to lower levels does not necessarily provide more information in the context of capacity management. As defined in this book, the lowest levels of capacity that exist are space, labor, equipment, IT, and materials.

Space

Space capacity represents the physical locations that a firm has secured, and often it is where a firm's work is performed. Fundamentally, this represents the offices where the firm operates. It will also include the manufacturing facilities, office space, and its warehouses. It includes the trucks that an organization owns or to which it has access; anything with a usable square footage represents the space of an organization. The critical issues for managing space as an entity is how much space is necessary to perform the necessary work. Too much space might result in paying too much for the capacity. "Might" is used here because reducing this space may or may not result in cost reduction. For example, if an organization reduces its office space used from 10,000 square feet to 9,000 square feet but it still pays for the 10,000 square feet, there have been no real cost savings.

Space competence will be very important as an organization figures out how much space will be required to perform its activities. The effective utilization of space may or may not lower costs, however; if organizations manage their space effectively, they can create decision options or degrees of freedom that allow the firm to improve its financial performance. Firms with strong space competence can figure out what levels of space are necessary and plan their output accordingly. They can also use this competence to figure out how to increase their output in existing space, leading to increased margins.

The confusing aspect of managing space is trying to figure out just how much space is required to meet expected demand. Additional details will be discussed in Chapter 3, but the essential criteria are based on what occurs in the space and on the competence of the constitutive components making up the processes. Competence determines the elasticity that in this case, controls how space increases or decreases will be managed. For example, organizations that manage space poorly require faster rates of capacity increase, given increased product or service demand, than those who are more competent. Competent organizations may be able to stretch the existing available capacity, which may lead to improved financial returns. Simply, for the more competent firm, the costs increase at a slower rate than the revenues leading to increased profitability.

Labor

Labor capacity represents the amount of labor that an organization employs to perform work. The labor will include the traditional definitions of direct labor and indirect labor. Traditional definitions of both types of labor here are, relatively speaking, irrelevant from a macro level but become more relevant at a more micro level. At a macro level, as an organization seeks to understand the overall size of its labor capacity, what one does is not relevant. This view only gives a snapshot that allows one to understand ultimately the relative sizes of organizations. There are measures and metrics, such as sales per person or sales per capacity unit; however, such metrics do not give an organization an understanding of *where* they are stronger or weaker than their competition, as it relates to capacity management. Organizational operations and processes are too different, and the ratios often too easily manipulated, for such measures to be meaningful. Additionally, they are likely to be at too high a level to provide useful information.

The net result, therefore, is that an organization must have a more granular understanding of their labor capacity. For management purposes, as discussed in Chapters 6 and 7, it will be important for organizations to understand to what their capacity is allocated to understand the capacity requirements of operations and processes. This will provide the information basis that should be used for benchmarking and performance improvement purposes.

Fundamentally, the amount of labor capacity in time is equal to the sum of the individuals in the organization and the hours that each individual works. This will help the organization understand how much total labor capacity is available. Time is important here because it is the primary criterion that should be used to manage labor capacity. All other labor-related measures, such as output rate, will be a direct function of the labor hours that are available to be worked.

31

Equipment

In this book, equipment is synonymous with machines and machine technology. Information technology will be covered independently as *technology* in the next section. Machines will include equipment used to make products and used primarily in manufacturing-type environments. They may also be used in certain service industries, such as restaurants, where the service, which is really a product such as food, is manufactured.

Each individual piece of equipment has its own capacity. At a maximum, it is determined by its top speed, multiplied by the number of hours in operations. So a machine capable of processing 10 units per hour for an 8-hour shift has a theoretical capacity of 80 units per shift. Clearly, other issues affect its ability to produce at a maximum level, and many of these are discussed in Chapter 3.

As an entity, the theoretical capacity for equipment is somewhat easy to determine. Equipment capacity becomes more difficult to manage as one begins creating operations and processes for analysis and management. The capacity of the operation depends, for example, on whether the entities operate within a process in series or in parallel, the capacity of upstream and downstream operations, or on whether the machine operators are available.

Information Technology

Information technology capacity represents the capacity of an organization's computing resources to perform various types of data and information-related functions. From a networking perspective, the capacity represents the amount of data that can be transmitted per unit of time. From a processing perspective, it represents the number of transactions or tasks that can be carried out in a period of time. From a storage perspective, capacity represents the amount of data that can be stored in the organization's IT resources. Determining and understanding IT capacity is very important as one begins to understand how computers can be used for work.

Networks with limited capacity ultimately constrain the number of bytes of data that can be performed per unit of time. Once the capacity reaches its maximum level, the time involved to perform the transactions increases due to the time involved while waiting to be processed. The same issue arises when looking at the processing capabilities of IT resources. Some tasks utilize large amounts of IT resources. Scientific and technical computing activities are notorious for using processing capacity. Computers that process a large number of transactions see a decrease in performance when the transactions require processing at the same time. As the number of transactions increases, the total lead time it takes to accomplish a task can increase, leading to a reduced ability for work to be performed quickly.

Material

Viewing material as capacity is a somewhat nontraditional way of looking at inventory. However, inventory in certain forms is exactly that, capacity. Material capacity represents the inventory that an organization has to meet anticipated demand. Theoretically, the quantity of materials that the organization has and the required number of units for each finished product determine this material capacity. Therefore, an organization with twelve tires has the capacity to make three automobiles.

Looking at inventory as capacity is very beneficial for two reasons:

- It provides a way of managing inventory that frees the organization from tying inventory directly to products. Such separation allows organizations to begin to identify material decisions that negatively impact financial statements.

- It allows the organization to consider combining various types of capacity, which now includes materials, to get work done. The organization can plan tasks and operations more easily.

Operational Capacity

The previous section focused on defining entities. The entities are combined to create operations or operational capabilities. The purpose of combining entities into operations is that the capabilities of the entities are enhanced and new capabilities and competencies are created. This can ultimately lead to the creation of products and services that the organization is going to provide. This enhancement is created by the interactions of the entities. A person can, for instance, create the perception of having an increased knowledge base by having the right IT capacity at his or her fingertips. The capacity of the individual has remained the same, but the capability and competence has increased as a result of getting access to more data or information. This person-IT relationship is an example of a *heterogeneous capacity combination.* When creating combinations of entities, either of two combinations can be created: homogeneous combinations or heterogeneous combinations. With *homogeneous combinations*, changes to competence may or may not take place. The primary emphasis is on increasing the baseline capacity. Combinations of like components linearly increase the capacity of the components. For example, if an organization's space capacity in one building is 10,000 square feet and it buys another building with 10,000 square feet, its capacity became the sum of the two. Its competence does not increase as a result of the interaction. The objective of heterogeneous combinations is to create increased competence rather than increased capacity (see Exhibit 2.1). A building that is combined with the right equipment may create manufacturing abilities that may not exist otherwise.

There are 15 entity-entity combination possibilities (see Exhibit 2.2). It is important to note that not all entity-entity combinations create operations. Two buildings do not make an operation. Two materials do not make an operation. Two pieces of equipment do not make an operation. In these cases, just having the entities does not lead to work

EXHIBIT 2.1

Type of combination determines the resulting improvement in the organization.

Type of Combinations	Competence	Capacity
Homogeneous	Same	Increases
Heterogeneous	Increases	Same

being finished. Two people may be able to create an operation, as might two IT systems. In these cases, sharing data or information to make decisions can occur, which can be the basis for certain types of operations.

Homogeneous Capacity

Homogeneous capacity is created as a result of combining like entities. By definition, there are five different types of homogenous capacity combinations:

- Space-space
- Labor-labor
- Equipment–equipment
- IT-IT
- Material-material

EXHIBIT 2.2

Five of the entity-entity combinations are homogeneous, whereas the remaining ten are heterogeneous.

	Space	Labor	Equipment	IT	Materials
Space	S-S	S-L	S-E	S-I	S-M
Labor		L-L	L-E	L-I	L-M
Equipment			E-E	E-I	E-M
IT				I-I	I-M
Materials					M-M

In all five cases, the suggestion is that combining like entities will lead to benefits that primarily increase capacity, although it will increase competence on occasion (see Exhibit 2.3). The reason is simply that the interactions often do not involve different competencies, each of which would be enhanced as a result of the interaction. So, adding another building to an existing building complex allows for the firm to bring in more labor, equipment, IT, and materials but will not itself improve the individual processes and activities that occur.

Space-Space Capacity

The benefits that one achieves from secondary spatial capacity depend on the type of space being combined. If space, for some reason, constrains growth, the additional space may relieve the constraints that would lead to increased growth but will not add to the competence that the organization currently has. Processes will still perform as before. The relative capabilities and knowledge that influence people policies, processes, and technologies have not changed. The amount of space in which they perform their functions has changed. This concept is the same, whether the organization adds warehouse space, office space, or factory space.

Labor-Labor Capacity

Adding labor capacity, regardless of its source, increases the number of labor hours that an organization has to perform its work. So, whether adding an accounts payable clerk or a direct labor factory worker, the organization has increased its total available hours to perform some type of work. This says nothing to competence, however. Having the factory worker perform accounts-payable transactions and having payables clerks run a machining center may not lead to the desired output from either operation. This is a management issue and not a capacity issue. The increased organizational competence results from management properly applying labor to a task or operation.

EXHIBIT 2.3

Homogeneous combinations of entities create increases in capacity of the entity, but in some cases can create the potential for competence improvement within the firm.

Entity	Benefit
Space	Additional area (square feet or square meters), facilitate other interactions
Labor	Additional time, interactions can create more knowledge
Equipment	Additional processing time and capabilities
IT	Additional processing capabilities and transaction flexibility
Material	Additional processing capacity and range of products

Adding labor capacity may, however, increase organizational competence. Notice that the statement suggests that competence may or may not increase. It all depends on the nature and type of labor capacity that is being added. One positive aspect of labor capacity is its knowledge. People have the capability to share knowledge and learn. This knowledge, whether gained or shared, may increase the capabilities of the organization: the CEO who has built organizations; the engineers who share products development ideas; the factory workers who talk about improved methods. In all cases, the person being added to the organization, whether CEO, engineer, or factory worker, has the ability to increase the competence of the organization. Consequently, the increase in competence results from adding the right people to the right people, so that improvements will occur as a result of the interactions.

Equipment-Equipment Capacity

Adding equipment is conceptually similar to adding space capacity, except for the fact that machines tend to be much more specialized in their use.

So, while an organization may purchase a warehouse and convert it into office space or factory space, a multi-axis machining center will never become a punch press. Therefore, although the capacity is increased incrementally by the capacity of the equipment, it may also increase the competence of the organization's equipment capacity. To say arbitrarily that the competence has increased as a result of increased equipment would be somewhat irresponsible. One must assess what the capacity adds and then determine the impact on competence.

IT-IT Capacity

IT capacity is very similar to space capacity but to a different extent than equipment. IT, like some machines, can be very specialized. Although certain application architectures run better on certain types of hardware, many applications can be ported to run on various operating systems using various languages on multiple hardware platforms.

Information technology can increase the competence of an organization, but significant increases in competence result from either fully integrated capabilities or specialized computers and applications. Increases in competence resulting from integrating solutions are created by allowing systems to share data and information and to allow workflow capabilities to be incorporated, therefore improving the decision-making and operational components of the process. For example, a customer service software solution may be able to provide better information when combined with client information from a sales automation system. The customer service solution will know what the customer has purchased, when, what contracts might be in place, key customer contacts, and so on. This information may not naturally exist in the customer service system if the people responsible for customer service do not have access to this information or have historically not operated in this way. If the information were to exist, it may be inaccurate if the information had been gained from people who are not fully knowledgeable of all of the interactions between the two companies.

Specialized computers can provide new competencies altogether. An organization that designs products without sufficient computing capacity and competence will likely benefit from competence that allows them to build models and test their performance in a high-powered computing system. Products, such as fighter airplanes, can be designed and tested in computers that help engineers learn more about the interaction between design and flight dynamics than ever before. A change can be made and the aircraft retested in the software before a full-scale working prototype is ever created. Before, such extensive testing and refining might have been prohibitively expensive.

Material-Material Capacity

Adding materials is practically the same as adding space. The way that they are the same is that, by adding materials, one basically adds to what can be made. However, it is not completely true in all circumstances. For example, having 12 tires allows a factory to make 3 cars. Having 16 tires allows the factory to make 4 cars. Having 14 tires does nothing for the factory, other than allowing it to buy fewer tires in the future.

Arguably, adding material may, in some way, add to the organization's competence. If the organization has the labor competence and equipment competence, it can take special materials and make products that cannot be made in other environments. This might lead to the argument that the competence is added at either the operational or process levels where increases in organizational competence result from creating interactions with dissimilar capacity. Material by itself increases the number of products that can be made. An organization may buy titanium and choose to make cheap trash cans. It is their choice. Therefore, fundamentally, capacity competence has not been increased.

Homogeneous capacity components in general add the ability to increase the amount of work that can be done and not the complexity or variability of what can be made. Increases in competence will more likely result in combinations created by heterogeneous capacity types.

Heterogeneous Secondary-Capacity Types

Ten of the fifteen capacity types are heterogeneous, which makes up the remaining permutations of entity-entity relationships. When the situation occurs where heterogeneous entities combine, two things can occur:

- Capacity of both are changed.
- Competence increases as a result of the interaction.

Capacity Expectation

The expectations from a capacity perspective are fairly simple to describe. Each entity brings something to the combination that improves what either could do independently. A person (labor) and a machine (equipment), for instance, are able to perform various functions independently. The machine is capable of processing parts of an assumed rate of 8 units per hour. Without an operator, however, it may not be able to process any units at all. With a person added to it working an 8-hour shift, the expectation is that the combination can process 64 units per shift. The output that is expected from the machine itself has changed. By itself, its capabilities are limited. With labor added, its operation rate is now realizable. Labor, too, is more capable. It can now make products that it is incapable of producing without the equipment.

What would keep the expected capacity from being reached is one or both components failing to deliver on its capacity capability. If the person were to work 7 hours, only 56 units will be produced. If the machine broke down, or for some reason it was unable to operate at the sustained rate of 8 units per hour, the expected output would not be met.

All in all, entities can come together to help perform the work tasks that are required of the organization. Labor and IT come together to design products, invoice customers, and manage inventory. IT and equipment come together to automate manufacturing processes and to enable information sharing among the equipment. Space and labor come together to provide offices and office workers who perform work daily. As we should now see, it is the operational, process, and organizational levels that allow for true work and work tasks to be performed.

Competence Increases

The work tasks that are performed and the efficiency with which they are performed are all functions of the competence of the capacity. An example of how entities come together is automobile racing. Assume that there are two drivers, Spike and Ike, who race for the same team. Assume, additionally, that the cars in which they race are identically prepared, suggesting that the cars have the same fundamental components. The speed that either has will be based on his natural talent, how he sets up the car (e.g., higher or lower downforce), how he interacts with the car, the particular track, and the weather conditions. These five components in this simplified case will help determine the capacity competence created between driver and car.

Assume that Spike is faster in all conditions. The competence created between Spike and his car is greater. The car by itself is not a factor because without a driver, it is not able to do anything. Spike's speed does not exist without a car, so the ability is created when the two interact. Spike knows, whether intellectually, physically, or both, how to work with his car more effectively. He understands how to get the car to handle the way he wants it to handle. So, even if he may not be the faster of the two drivers based on natural talent alone, Spike may know what he has to do to be faster—to increase his competence.

Assume that Ike may be faster in some circumstances. There will be numerous reasons for this, such as Ike can drive better in the rain or Ike likes much more technical race courses than Spike. The combination with the highest competence in this case may be determined by the situation. On nontechnical courses with no rain, Spike may be more competent. In technical courses with rain, Ike may be more competent.

Organizational capacity competence operates similarly. The competence of the operation is determined by bringing together the entities. Certain entities will create higher competence, and some will create competencies that are not as great. In Chapter 3, where the focus is on measuring capacity, the issue will be discussed in more depth. The competence may also be situation–dependent. Some organizations may operate more effectively in certain environments or situations than others. Competence is a very important issue to manage, so that your organization knows its strengths and weaknesses, so that the right strategies and tactical acivities can be implemented to improve overall performance.

The next section will focus on bringing together heterogeneous entities to create operational capacity. As mentioned previously, there are ten mutually exclusive, heterogeneous entity combinations (see Exhibit 2.4). Each will be discussed in turn.

EXHIBIT 2.4

Heterogeneous combinations make up most of the operational capacity types that will exist.

	Space	Labor	Equipment	IT	Materials
Space		S-L	S-E	S-I	S-M
Labor			L-E	L-I	L-M
Equipment				E-I	E-M
IT					I-M
Materials					

Space-Labor Capacity

Space-labor interactions involve people working in a space, whatever that space may be. So, the space may involve white collar workers in an office or blue collar workers in a factory. In either case, the emphasis is on ensuring the desired level of competence when bringing together the two. For example, incompetent people will fail, regardless of the space in which they work. Competent people may fail to reach their potential if they are working in a suboptimal space. Space-labor capacity involves ensuring the greatest likelihood of overall success for the organization. Location is often critical, as having the right people at the right place can increase an organization's ability to serve its customers. Additionally, certain geographies, political regions, and educational regions are more conducive to certain industries or markets. Workers within certain geographies with certain competencies may allow for advanced economic growth within the region, as has been seen in areas, such as Pittsburgh with steel and Silicon Valley with technology.

Space-Equipment Capacity

Space-equipment interactions create the ability to make products within a space. An example would be a factory where equipment is laid out with the intention of being able to make products. Objectives here often involve effectively laying out the equipment, so that the desired capacity and competence can be achieved in the least amount of space.

Space-IT Capacity

Space-IT interactions are fairly straightforward. They involve space utilized by IT equipment. This has become an issue with many organizations, as having many smaller computers will take up large amounts of space, especially with the advent of Internet technologies, which have supported the need to place personal computers on practically every

IN THE REAL WORLD

Toyota Production System

As necessity is the mother of invention, lack of space and the need for productivity have a major influence on the Toyota Production System, also known as *just-in-time manufacturing*. Japan, being approximately the size of California, is only 20% habitable and has approximately half of the population of the United States. In addition, at the time, Toyota found itself well behind the other major automobile manufacturers throughout the world. With no extra space and a lack of productivity, Toyota was able to design a system that improved equipment-space capacity and competence in ways that the world had never seen. With an inability (and some would argue lack of desire) to run large batch sizes due to space constraints, Toyota developed the ultimate small-batch manufacturing system, with equipment placed close to each other, along with the ability to perform quick changeovers. They also found the "U"-configuration of equipment where entire processes were arranged in a "U"-shape to increase productivity, as well. With this shape came the ability for a worker to easily manage multiple machines by working within the "U" itself. The result was a system that utilized much less space than traditional systems, could operate with lower capacity levels, and was much more responsive than traditional manufacturing operations.

desk. Many organizations find that the IT space is not being used effectively, leading to the potential for increased space-related costs. The issue of competence occurs as a result. Can other organizations with whom one competes get more from their space-IT interactions? Does an organization require more systems to accomplish work, given space constraints? Or does one organization require more space to house IT capacity? Additional space, however, might help increase the competence of the organization by allowing for special technologies to be adopted.

Space-Materials Capacity

Space-materials capacity involves the utilization of space by materials. There are two issues to consider regarding space and materials. The first is that organizations do not want the storage of materials to utilize too much space. Ineffective storage techniques can lead to the overutilization of space. The amount of materials stored should align as closely to actual demand as possible. Additionally, it is desirable to minimize space occupied while ensuring that it is properly located, so as to support effective and efficient manufacturing practices. The latter is difficult to perform without an effective cost-benefit analysis occurring.

The second issue is whether space can provide another type of competitive advantage. The amount of space available might support an organization's ability to store specialty materials, therefore potentially increasing the organization's competence. The other is the location of the space. Having the space in the right geographic location may allow organizations to respond to customer demand more quickly or at a lower cost. Inventory location can, in some cases, be an often-overlooked opportunity to improve organizational and financial performance.

Labor-Equipment Capacity

Labor-equipment capacity gives an organization the ability to build the products that it sells. Oftentimes, labor is required to operate equipment, whether for the actual operation of the equipment, maintaining the equipment, or scheduling work on the equipment. For manufacturing organizations, this interaction is very important because the livelihood of the firm rests on its ability to generate revenue through its products while managing costs.

As seen with Spike and Ike, the competence of the labor capacity can have a major impact on the overall labor-equipment capacity. For example, in many cases, automatic machines create the opportunity for one person to manage multiple machines. The operator can start one machine and then step over to another and prepare it for operation. In a more traditional manual environment, two people would likely be necessary to run the two machines. The knowledge of how labor interacts with the right type of equipment can give the organization this type of advantage. As will be seen in Chapters 3 and 7, measuring and optimizing this interaction will actually require organizations to reconsider some of the tasks being performed or the rate at which they are performed. Without a complete understanding of labor-equipment capacity and how to measure it, organizations can find themselves making mistakes that can negatively impact their operational and financial performance.

Labor-IT Capacity

Labor and IT represent the capabilities that are created when people and IT systems/software interact. The result can often be wonderful, but it can also be disappointing. From a positive perspective, the competence that can result from the proper implementation and use of information technology can lead to discoveries that improve products and service. The capacity and capacity competence can lead to processes with operations that approach an optimized state. Processes can be more efficient and effective. From a negative perspective, one often sees organizations that invest in the technology but do not achieve much of the financial and operational benefits. Organizations implement solutions that are not integrated or that are difficult to adapt to the normal operations of the organization. Similarly, organizations with the improper leadership in place experience poor adaptation rates.

Labor-Materials Capacity

On the surface, the interactions of labor and materials seem quite simple. People have a certain capacity and, when coupled with materials, create the ability to produce a number of products. However, this is only a part of the story. Labor competence can highly influence both what can be made and the amount of material required to make it.

Highly competent labor might be able to process materials that others may find difficult or impossible to process. This might also be a function of equipment competence, as well, but let us assume that the equipment is the same. The knowledge of the material and the issues that arise from its processing can often go a long way in designing and developing the right operations and processes. Highly competent workers might be able to work with specialized materials and often utilize fewer materials to provide similar output. With specialized materials, higher-valued items can be created. With higher rates of quality and more effective utilization of materials comes less wasted material. Poor quality processes require more materials to get the desired number of parts. For example, a poor-quality process may require 110 components to make 100 good parts, whereas a high-quality process may only require 101. In this case, the capacity of 500 units in inventory increases.

Equipment-IT Capacity

The interaction of equipment and IT provides organizations with the ability to increase the competence of the equipment capacity. First, IT technologies allow equipment to *communicate* with each other. One piece of equipment can "tell" another on what it just operated, so that the subsequent piece of equipment can download the right processing program. These are decisions that, at one time, were reserved for individuals to make as they scheduled, planned, and set up the equipment.

IT and equipment can also increase capacity and competence through the application of optimization and simulation software. Optimization software can focus on the efficient and effective utilization of time and/or materials. The optimization tools can focus on how equipment uses materials, which can lead to insight that can ultimately reduce material requirements and costs. Optimization can also help with order sequencing and equipment scheduling, so that the desired performance and financial expectations are met.

Equipment-Material Capacity

Equipment and materials come together to make products. The combination of the two creates the capacity. One hundred units per hour with 500 units in inventory lead to a capacity of 5 hours. The equipment-material capacity combination is a tricky one to manage; one must balance equipment utilization and demand, inventory levels and demand, and inventory levels and equipment utilization.

These perspectives must all be managed and are often managed with tools that provide inadequate solutions. Manufacturing consultants still find situations where organizations build inventory to ensure the utilization of equipment, even though demand does not exist. The net result is that machines are utilized, but the investment in inventory often yields less-than-desirable results. The inventory is not generating revenue for the organization and the cash is unable to be invested elsewhere for greater returns.

The issues discussed here will be addressed in more detail later in Chapters 6 and 7. Clearly, for manufacturing organizations, this becomes an important issue and one that requires a significant amount of guidance to ensure optimal operational and financial performance.

IT-Materials Capacity

The final heterogeneous operation combines information technology and materials. IT can be used to forecast demand more effectively and to provide information that can help optimize inventory levels, subject to existing defined constraints, such as space, time, and costs. IT has been, and will be, an important component, as organizations try to balance that which creates the aforementioned constraints. For example, a manufacturing organization must balance customer service levels with cost, capital management, and brand. In my almost two decades of working and consulting for manufacturing organizations, I have not seen an organization that fully understands and acts on the understanding to potentially reduce service levels so as to improve the overall financial and operational aspects of the organization. Most organizations forgo the financial benefits and carry too much inventory, so that the customer service levels can be increased.

Combining More Than Two Entities

Operational-functional combinations can exist at an order greater than two (a pair). For simplicity, and as an introduction to the topic, pairs or second-order capacity combinations were discussed. However, third-order and higher-order groupings can exist. A person on his or her computer in a room with no other context is a third-order functional combination. The key criterion to consider when defining a functional grouping is the question, does this grouping perform a process, or not? If not, it will be a functional combination whose role is to work with other functional combinations to perform a process.

Process capacity represents the combination of multiple entities and/or operational-functional groups to perform a specific type of work. An example might be an accounting office. Space (office) is combined with multiple labor-IT pairs to create the ability to process invoices and make payments. The combination of all three with organizational rules provides the compatibility necessary to create a process. The combinations and permutations of pairs and triplets in this case are practically infinite until narrowing down a specific organization and its specific entities. One organization with X buildings, each with Y computers and Z people to operate them, have N possible ways to combine space, labor, and IT. It is only when we narrow

Joe down to a specific building that we can begin to manage the process easily. Joe in Portland can perform his job on any of the ten computers. At this point, capacity issues are much more easily managed and understood.

Processes are probably the key criterion to consider when managing capacity. Although individual entities are important, it is when they are called on by the organization that this importance in this context is realized. The same holds true for operational-functional combinations. Therefore, detailed discussion about process management will begin in Chapter 4 and will continue throughout the book.

Organizational capacity combines multiple processes to assess its ability to operate synchronously. Although organizations may have strong individual process combinations, the processes may not effectively interact, which may lead to a suboptimal organization. The main objective is an organization with optimal operating and/or financial performance. This means that the processes must not only work, they must work well together to provide what is necessary to achieve desired results.

TIPS & TECHNIQUES

- What types of capacity entities and operations are most important to your organization?

- Consider whether there is enough of an understanding of how entities come together to make processes. What types of mistakes are being made regarding how operations are being managed?

- When you make entity and operations-related decisions, make sure that the organization is increasing its capacity and competence to the greatest extent possible.

Summary

This chapter focused on the type of capacity that exists in an organization. The primary capacity, or the entity, introduced space, labor, equipment, IT, and materials as the building blocks of capacity. Secondary, or operational/functional, capacity, combines the entities into combinations, which have the ability to carry out tasks or operations. The tertiary, or process, level combines functional groupings and turns them into a process capable of performing some type of work. Finally, the quaternary, or organizational, level, brings together many processes to define the overall capabilities of the organization.

The next chapter will introduce measurements. Before combining entities, operations, and processes, the fundamentals of measuring must be introduced, so that management and improvement of the resulting groupings is achievable.

Endnotes

[1] Eliyahu Goldratt and Jeff Cox, *The Goal: A Process of Ongoing Improvement*, Revised Edition (Croton-on-Hudson, N.Y.: North River Press, 1986).

CHAPTER 3

Measuring Capacity

After reading this chapter you will be able to:

- Articulate the base measures of capacity
- Articulate and discuss the six types of measures used for operations
- Understand how the operations measures can be used to measure operation output
- Understand which levers to adjust to get more or less output from the operations

Measurements

Now that capacity has been defined, the next critical step is to discuss how to measure capacity. Correctly measuring capacity is a sine qua non for managing capacity because the decisions made when managing capacity are often based on the measurements that one observes. For example, ineffectively utilizing space might cause a manager to improve its utilization to more effective levels.

The measurement concepts have to reflect and represent all of the types of capacity that exist. From entity capacity through organizational capacity, the approach must support any combination that one may encounter. This chapter introduces the capacity management approach that will be used for the rest of the book. The system is based on four primary capacity components:

- Area/volume
- Operations/tasks
- Products
- Time

Area/Volume

Area[1] is a primary measure that is usually attributed to space capacity. Area represents a two-dimensional space and will therefore be measured in squared-length units, such as square feet, square meters, or square centimeters. Area can also be attributed to the other capacity entities, as well. This is due to the fact that every other capacity component that utilizes available space takes up space. This is not to be confused with space capacity. Rather, the space measurement will impact the utilization and availability of capacity, as well as capacity decisions regarding capacity requirements.

Operations/Tasks

Operations and tasks represent the number of actions that can be performed. At this point, it only represents the total number (transactions) and not the frequency (tasks ÷ time). This is because transactions per hour is a secondary measure that involves the combination of two primary measures (operations and time). Operations are somewhat tricky because, unlike area, they can vary by what is being processed. In other words, often there are no basic standards for operations, even when using the same equipment. The same piece of equipment, for example, is likely to process different products differently. Additionally, the nature of operating suggests that natural variability will exist. Realized output will tend to vary from the rated or expected operational measures based on operating conditions, such as operator competence.

Item/Products

The item or the product represents material capacity to perform work. Items or products can be measured depending on the usage. For example, if a material is used for multiple products in varying quantities, it is very difficult, if not impossible, to measure the products that can be created without allocating the material. The allocation may or may not be arbitrary. It is similar to trying to predict the number of miles that can be traveled from a tank of gas. There are many variables to consider that can impact what the actual value will be. An average can be taken, but this does not help when the actual number is below the average leaving the driver stranded on the freeway. If the item is used in one product or in constant ratios, such as having four tires on a car, the number of products that can be created is determinable. Otherwise, items should be used as the base measure. For the rest of this discussion, the emphasis will be placed on the product because determining its value as a capacity measure is less intuitive and less common.

The number of products that can be created is a capacity measurement for most materials and will be a primary measure for operations and processes. For example, if a facility has 20,000 tires in its warehouse, this is enough capacity to create 5,000 cars, assuming cars do not get spares. Products, too, can vary, depending on process or the type of material being used. With high-quality processes or with software that optimizes the use of materials, one might be able to impact the number of products that can be created with a given amount of materials. Optimal processes cannot get 5,001 cars from 20,000 tires. However, it might be able to get more body parts for the vehicle with the same amount of steel going into processing.

Material type can also make a difference. Poor-quality materials may fail in production or require a greater quantity in the process than higher-quality materials.

Time

Time itself is clearly unalterable. What is alterable, however, is the overall availability and utilization of capacity. A capacity unit or capacity type may be available for a full 24-hour process or some portion less. Determining the amount of time that is actually available for work or used for work will lead to the use of measures such as availability and utilization. These concepts are briefly discussed here and revisited in Chapter 5.

Availability

Availability represents the amount of time that capacity is theoretically available. For example, equipment might be available for 24 hours each day. Labor, however, may only be available for 10 hours each day. The labor availability will limit or constrain the equipment availability to 10 hours each day if the equipment needs labor to operate. Availability is a critical criterion for being able to understand how capacity is being used because it is the basis for the other utilization and efficiency measures upon which many decisions are made.

availability = amount of time available to perform work

Utilization

Utilization represents the percentage of available time that a resource is being used. For example, if a resource is available for 10 hours, but is doing work for 5 of the 10 hours, it is said to be 50% utilized.

utilization = time used for value adding work ÷ available time

No judgment will be made regarding utilization, except for the following. Higher utilization does not arbitrarily mean more effective operations. As will be discussed in Chapter 5 and beyond, utilization should be a function of the conditions in which the resource is operating, such as demand being placed on it and its overall role within a process. This is a very important concept that will be reiterated throughout the book.

By applying availability and utilization, one can begin to understand the time capacity that resources will have. This is critical when ultimately considering the number of tasks that can occur versus the number of tasks that need to occur. This will create an understanding of where there might be too much capacity or not enough capacity.

Summarizing, all of the capacity measures that can ultimately be created are based on the primary measures. Each capacity entity will be tied to either a single basic measure or multiple basic measures based on what the entity is capable of doing or impacting (see Exhibit 3.1). For example, space is an area measure, but labor can be time (hours worked), area (physical space required), and operations (competence of an individual to perform the job). The next section will focus on combining entities to create operations-type measures.

EXHIBIT 3.1

Each capacity entity has primary measures that can be used to measure its capacity.

Capacity Entity	Primary Measures
Space	Area
Labor	Time, area, operations
Equipment	Operations, time, area
IT	Operations, time, area
Materials	Products, area

Second-Order Measures

As capacity types are combined, different types of measures must exist to determine their capacity. For example, labor and equipment have the same primary measures. However, determining the value of the combined capacity is not simply a function of considering the time measure for one or the other due to the interactions between the entities. The interaction creates a different value when the two are combined, and the resulting output of their combined efforts must be measured. Combining them, therefore, requires measures that consider the interactions between the entities and can accurately provide the information needed to understand or manage the process.

There are six second-order measures for capacity:

1. Products-time (e.g., products per minute)

2. Area-time (e.g., square ft per year)

3. Operations-time (e.g., units per hour)

4. Operations-area (e.g., tasks per square ft)

5. Operations-product (e.g., operations per unit)

6. Area-product (e.g., square ft per unit)

 TIPS & TECHNIQUES

All operations and processes should have measures associated with them. The ideal values associated with these measures should be determined by role of the operation in the overall process and not by some other, arbitrary method.

Time-Products

Products and time represent the rate at which products can be made. The measure can either exist as a measure such as units per time (widgets/hour) or time per unit (hours/widget). An example might be a person who works an 8-hour shift each day operating a piece of equipment that handles an average of 10 units per hour. Ten units per hour translates into 1 unit every 6 minutes. On average, one can expect that the combination will create a total of 80 units per day.

Throughput of this type of capacity is impacted by:

- Time limitations of capacity
- Operations limitations of capacity
- Competence of the capacity

Time Limitations

The total time available for processing capacity is impacted by availability and utilization. Equipment might be paired with labor that is only operational for one 8-hour shift. The 8-hour shift would limit the overall availability of the operation. If, for some reason, either resource is utilized 7 of the 8 hours, the total output will be reduced even further. It is irrelevant which resource creates the disruption when assessing the impact on output. The person may take breaks for an hour or the machine can break down for an hour. The net result of losing an hour is the same either way.

To reduce the impact of time as a constraint, one can improve availability, utilization, or both. Consider the organization with demand that exceeds the throughput of the operation. The demand, let us assume, is for 100 parts per day. Assume further that the operating cost consists of one person who works for one 8-hour shift on a machine capable of operating at a rate of 10 units per hour. Assume further that the machine has all 8 hours available to process. The maximum theoretical throughput of this particular operation is determined by Equation 3.1.

$$\frac{parts}{hour} \times \frac{hours}{day} \times utilization = \frac{parts}{day}$$

$$\frac{10 \text{ parts}}{hour} \times \frac{8 \text{ hours}}{day} \times 100\% \text{ utilization} = \frac{80 \text{ parts}}{day}$$

3.1

Although at a maximum, the process does not meet the demands of the market. Once true utilization is factored in, the situation may become worse. Assume that poor maintenance leads to downtime equal to 2 hours per day. The result is now a utilization of 75% (see Equation 3.2), leading to a reduction in the total parts per hour (see Equation 3.3).

$$utilization = \frac{hours\ worked}{hours\ available}$$

$$= \frac{6 \text{ hours worked}}{8 \text{ hours available}}$$

$$= 75\%$$

3.2

$$\frac{parts}{day} = \frac{parts}{hour} \times \frac{hours}{day} \times utilization$$

$$\frac{60 \text{ parts}}{day} = \frac{10 \text{ parts}}{hour} \times \frac{8 \text{ hours}}{day} \times 0.75$$

3.3

For this particular situation, the organization would want to focus on achieving maximum utilization. If it pays for 8 hours yet gets the output of 6 hours, the organization is sacrificing revenues.

The organization will likely want to come as close to 100 units as possible without significantly increasing its costs. For example, one option might be to bring in a resource to work another shift to increase availability. In this case, one doubles the operating costs (1 person to 2 people), yet the maximum sellable output increases by only 25%. Remember, there is only demand for 100 units, so the organization only needs 20 more units, assuming 100% utilization. Doubling operating costs while increasing revenue by 25% is not a recipe for long-term survival.

Operations Limitations

Operation-time measures can be limited by the capability of the capacity, as well. Capacity will have its natural physical limits. A machine can only handle so many units, for example. Sometimes the limitations are based on physics and sometimes they are based on the design of the equipment. Physics limitations occur when considering issues, such as the transformation of materials or the physical limitations of the equipment, or the process, such as when materials are being heat-treated. With regard to design, certain equipment is just faster or more capable than other equipment. Hence, an older piece of equipment may process 10 units per hours, while a newer piece of equipment is able to process at 15, 20, or 25 units per hour. This would translate to fewer units-per-day values for the older equipment than for the newer equipment.

Competence Limitations

Assume that two people are operating the same piece of equipment. It is often the case that one operator might be more competent with the equipment than the other. For whatever reasons, and there may be many, the faster worker will create greater output with all things being equal. Therefore, the competence of the slow worker vis-à-vis the faster worker explains the lower output rate.

Managers have multiple options available to them when managing time-products as an operational measure. This critical measure will be addressed in much more detail in Chapters 5 and 7. Increasing the capability of the capacity involves relieving whatever constrains the output. These capacity components become the critical capacity to manage.

Area-Time

Area-time measures focus on the amount of area needed over a given period of time. An example measure might be square feet used or required per month or per year. From a transactional perspective, this type of measure may not make sense because few consider space and time together as a particular metric. However, for transactional operations, or if someone were attempting to plan future space requirements for budgeting purposes, this particular measure is critical. Either an average weighted cost per area or actual rent, lease, or purchase prices, for example, will allow you to budget space requirements and tie them to financial requirements necessary to manage the organization.

When considering area-time capacity, an important criterion to consider would be how to manage the space utilization effectively and efficiently over time. The objective would be to use the minimum space required to meet business objectives. The objectives might be financially oriented, such as minimizing the total cost of storage. They might be operationally oriented, such as positioning storage space, so that mean delivery time to customers is shortest. It might be to have enough space to manage growth and, thus, inventory expectations. In either case, area-time can be a critical component when planning space utilization in the future.

As with all measures, one will seek to improve area-time. Area-time must have another context related to it. For example, from a financial perspective, area-time might have a *growth element* and a *containment element*. The growth element might take into account the revenue requirements over time and the space required to ensure that the desired levels of area will be in place to support these growth expectations. Such a strategy must include, but not be limited to, the investment strategy in space resources. One might carry too much space in the short term, for instance, because it is part of ensuring that the necessary space is available now and in the future. The containment element would focus on the minimum requirements necessary for meeting demand. The objective is to minimize space expansion to the greatest extent possible with a constraint representing growth being considered.

From an operational perspective, one will work to ensure that the desired levels of space are available. This will allow the organization to meet anticipated demand, whether considering a factory for building products or an office that provides consulting services. The organization will ultimately need to provide context from a demand perspective as a fundamental input into the decision-making process. Along with the other types of capacity, the other criterion to consider is not only how much space is available over time but how much space is considered reasonable. One can argue that the minimum space requirement might be the block of area that all employees standing together in a room occupy. There would clearly be concerns regarding quality of work life in an environment like this. Therefore, reasonable expectations from all sides must be considered.

Operations-Time

Operations-time is a capacity measure that can be considered a frequency measure because it measures the number of times a task or operation occurs in a period of time: how many stampings per minute, cuts per hour, invoices per day. It is a very important capacity measure because operations-time represents both the capabilities of equipment being used and, oftentimes, the competence of the operator. So, whereas some measures such as operations-products may be fixed, operations-time will vary. Even as organizations implement time standards to help ensure that the operators seek operational goals, there will still be natural variability and external issues that can have an overall impact on operations-time as a measure.

Operations-time represents the tasks that the capacity must perform, whether they are repeat tasks or a set of instructions executed once. In many cases, these operations may lead to the creation of products. Multiple operations, for instance, might lead to one product. An example might be a machine that performs a number of cuts and shaping operations on a piece of metal until it creates a salable product. There might be one operation that creates multiple products, as with stamping a piece of metal to create multiple products. A part that requires three operations from a particular machine will find that it creates more output capacity than a part that requires five equivalent operations, assuming constant operating rates. This is because the fewer operations for each unit leads to greater volume output if the operations for both products are similar. So, although the operations per unit of time measure may be constrained, what one achieves with the output varies relative to the products being created.

Operations-Area

Operations-area measures help an organization understand how much space is required to perform the cycles or tasks. For example, an organization with slow accounts receivables transactions that takes up the same amount of space as an organization that is much faster might result in less-than-desirable overall space performance. To increase the output, the organization might have to increase the number of capacity resources that perform the tasks and must therefore increase its space if the space utilization requirements remain the same. The other option would be to improve the space utilization requirements by improving the process.

The importance of operations-area measures becomes even more salient as products are considered. The context of the operations becomes relevant when products and their relation to operations are considered. The ability to produce some sort of product or service is what is ultimately desired. To get this information, therefore, one must tie operations or tasks to the creation of products or services. The creation of a conversion factor, such as operations ÷ product or operations ÷ service, is necessary to have an ultimate understanding of what the operations-area capacity is capable of providing for the organization. Thus, whether the slower organization mentioned in the receivables example does, in fact, lead to a less-than-desirable performance depends on the service or product it is creating. The organization performing fewer operations per unit time might be just as well off, if not better off, because its products or services may require fewer operations or tasks.

Operations-Products

Operations-products, or operations-services, measures emphasize the steps or tasks necessary to create a product or a service. It may take eight steps to assemble a product. It may require 27 operations to order and pay for a computer printer. These steps are extremely important to understand when trying to assess the relative level of activities required to make a product or perform a service. One relatively simple rule is to design products and services to be created using as few operations as possible. The value of the additional steps must be questioned if one company can perform the required operations in five steps versus another that does it in seven. There are times when more steps might add value, such as additional activities designed to ensure a higher quality. If additional steps are required, every effort should be made to ensure that they are absolutely necessary and, therefore, value-adding steps.

As organizations seek to design the processes necessary to make products or perform services, there is really no reason for the processes to have non–value-adding steps. As will be discussed in Chapter 7, even for capacity that does not constrain output or throughput, making these processes more efficient provides options to improve an organization that many optimization approaches or techniques will fail to identify. This is frequent because throughput-based optimization problems do not identify options or degrees of freedom that are created from efficiency. They are just not modeled to provide such information.

Area-Products

Products–area measures are about space utilization. Products–per–square–foot unit measures help organizations understand the output of products and how much area is required to achieve this output. This becomes a more important measurement when linked to time and cost. Organizations create processes to perform work that leads to desired output as the various types of capacity come together. The labor, materials, and equipment come together to make products and services. There are so many materials that are available to be processed. There are so many machines that could be used for processing purposes. There are so many people available to operate the machines. All of these create the capacity to create capacity, and each utilizes space. The objective is to determine which combinations of area–utilizing entities will provide the desired output, given the space limitations that may exist. When linked to time, the emphasis is on products–time. When tied to cost, one considers the cost created by the spatial requirements to provide the necessary product output.

Recap

Each of the measures just mentioned are the fundamental measures for combining capacity types. They represent all of the output-based measures that one can obtain about an operation. Operations as we will find in Chapters 4 and 5 involve combining multiple entities to create a capacity entity capable of creating a product or service. When planning or measuring operations, the fundamental measures and combinations thereof will provide managers with the information that is required to measure any entity, any operation, and ultimately any process.

The next section will discuss how everyday issues are addressed by combining capacity and capacity measures. It will discuss these issues:

- Space utilization

- Labor output

- Equipment output

- IT output

- Material output

Effective Use of Capacity Entities

Now that the fundamental capacity measures have been introduced, it is time to discuss them in the context of specific types of capacity. The purpose of this section will be to discuss how the fundamental measures come together to help one manage the capacity entities. This section is important because it will be the foundation for the operations and processes that will be defined beginning in Chapter 4. As one looks to define an operation comprised of labor and equipment, how will the measures for each impact one another?

Space Utilization

Effectively managing space utilization is important because space can be a large cost for certain types of organizations. Management must be able to balance the amount of space that is available for its operations with what the operations are capable of performing in the space. On one hand, the organization does not want to have too much space. There may be additional costs that are associated with having too much space. If purchasing by the square foot, for example, the price increases with more square feet and if this space is not fully used, the organization might save money by operating in a smaller space. On the other hand, however, if the space is too small, the people working within the space may not be as productive as they possibly could be. Quarters that are too close may infringe on the comfort, privacy, and operating space of employees, which can lead to lower productivity.

When deciding how to utilize space, organizations usually have a couple of options. One can start with trying to decide how much space is needed, given the demands placed on the organization. Another option is trying to figure out whether the space that currently exists is being effectively utilized to provide the maximum output to meet the demand. The former deals more with space acquisition and the latter focuses on decision-making with current space levels.

Space Requirements

To determine how much space is required, one must understand something about the demands being placed on that portion of the organization that will need the space. Whether a factory to make products and services or an office area for accounts receivable, the objective and the approach are the same. One must begin by understanding how demand or anticipated demand translates into space. The transformation is a fairly simple one.

Consider, for example, an organization that needs to purchase a factory. Anticipated demand is 500 products per day. The question is, how does one transform this demand into space capacity requirements?

$$\frac{ft^2}{day} = \frac{products}{day} \times \frac{operations}{products} \times \frac{ft^2}{operation} \qquad 3.4$$

As is apparent from Equation 3.4, various types of capacity measures must be brought together to convert demand to space. One may begin with an output measure, such as parts per day, which determines how much output is either being demanded or how much the organization is capable of producing. The operations-parts measures (operations ÷ products) is used to describe the overall capability of operations to create products. This is a function of how the products are designed for production and of the architecture of the equipment. Finally, the operations-space measures (ft^2 ÷ operations) reflects the total amount of operations-space capacity that exists by combining all equipment.

Using Equation 3.4, organizations can transfer demand into space and can also understand that which can influence, either positively or negatively, the final answer. For this case, assume that demand is 500 units/day. There are 20 operations on average for each unit, and that the organization requires an average of 0.5 operations per each square foot each day. The total amount of space required would be 20,000 ft², as found in Equation 3.5.

$$\frac{20,000 \text{ ft}^2}{\text{day}} = \frac{500 \text{ units}}{\text{day}} \times \frac{20 \text{ operations}}{\text{unit}} \times \frac{1 \text{ ft}^2}{0.5 \text{ operations}} \qquad 3.5$$

In this case, assume that the demand will not change. In what ways can the organization improve, leading to reduced area requirements? It must focus on one or both of two areas. It can either reduce the number of operations for each part or increase the number of operations per square foot each day. For example, if the organization can reduce the number of operations per unit from 20 to 15, the space requirements would drop fairly significantly (see Equation 3.6).

Effective product and process design can lead to fewer operations per part being required. By tying products and processes together more effectively, using techniques such as design for manufacturability, the organization might be able to reduce the number of square feet required (see Equation 3.6).

$$\frac{15,000 \text{ ft}^2}{\text{day}} = \frac{15 \text{ operations}}{\text{unit}} \times \frac{1 \text{ ft}^2}{\text{unit}} \times \frac{500 \text{ units}}{\text{day}} \qquad 3.6$$

As is apparent in Exhibit 3.2, every change of one operation per part impacts 1,000 square feet of factory space. There may not be a clear relationship regarding how the interactions influence spatial requirements when designing the product and the process, but the net impact can, in some circumstances, be significant.

EXHIBIT 3.2

Flow changes in operations affect space.

Improvement in operations/part (reduction)	Reduction in space required
1	1,000
2	2,000
5	5,000
10	10,000

By improving the number of operations required to create each part, the theoretical amount of space may be required. This is theoretical because many other components of the relationship must be assessed. The equipment options may be constrained to one type, for example, leaving the space utilization the same regardless of the operations per part required.

The other way that one can impact the amount of area needed is to increase the number of operations per square unit of space that can occur in the space. Increasing the overall output of the equipment can lead to a fairly substantial reduction in the amount of space required. From the original equation, assume that the total number of operations each day in 1 square foot is increased by 50%, from 0.5 to 0.75. The impact is a reduction of approximately 35% when the operations/part remains the same (Equation 3.7).

$$\frac{13,333.\overline{3} \text{ ft}^2}{\text{day}} = \frac{500 \text{ units}}{\text{day}} \times \frac{20 \text{ operations}}{\text{unit}} \times \frac{\text{ft}^2}{0.75 \text{ operations}} \qquad 3.7$$

Current Space Utilization

The other scenario involves an organization trying to determine whether it is using its space as effectively as it possibly could. In this case, the space equation is the same, but the unknown quantity in the equation is different, as is apparent in Equation 3.8. Assume that an organization has 20,000 square feet for operations. Assume that everything else described in the previous example is all the same. The resulting output is determined by Equation 3.9.

$$\frac{\text{output}}{\text{day}} = \frac{\text{operations}}{\text{space}} \times \frac{\text{parts}}{\text{operations}} \times \frac{\text{total space}}{\text{day}} \qquad 3.8$$

$$\frac{500 \text{ parts}}{\text{day}} = \frac{0.5 \text{ operations}}{\text{space}} \times \frac{1 \text{ part}}{20 \text{ operations}} \times \frac{20,000 \text{ ft}^2}{\text{day}} \qquad 3.9$$

Now assume that a competitor is able to produce 700 parts a day from its space. The question is, can the organization use its existing space to get the output necessary to compete against its rival?[2] If so, how would they achieve the improvement? To get an output of 700 parts/day, the organization has three levers that it can use: operations-space, which may be equipment related, parts-operations, which is process-related, and space. If space is not an option to consider, the organization can only look to the amount of capabilities of the equipment or the design of the products and the processes being used to make the products.

 TIPS & TECHNIQUES

Spatial requirements may not always be variable, as described. You must consider not only the micro trends of a machine or two but also the macro trends of how the space is utilized overall. For example, increasing the number of operations per square foot may not have an immediate impact when analyzing one piece of equipment in a space, since its size is constant. However, when laying out new space, or when considering obtaining more equipment, their operation rate can give a high-level understanding regarding how much output can be derived from the square footage used by the equipment.

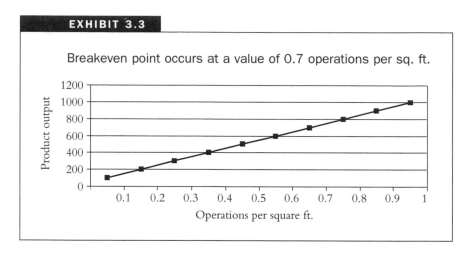

EXHIBIT 3.3

Breakeven point occurs at a value of 0.7 operations per sq. ft.

In this scenario, with space being the same, how would it get up to 700 units per day? If the organization focuses on operations per day space, holding operations per part constant for the sake of illustrating a particular point, there will be a clear breakeven point. This breakeven point can be determined algebraically and is seen in Exhibit 3.3. Any competence that exists where the organization can be capable of more than 0.7 operations per square foot each day will lead to an output greater than 700 units.

The organization must then consider how it would increase its ability to deliver some value equal to, or greater than, 0.7 operations per square foot each day. With the space being a constant, the only opportunity is to increase operations per sq. ft. Increasing operations per sq. ft. can happen in two ways: increasing the amount of equipment that provides the capability or increasing the capability of the equipment performing the work. Increasing the amount of equipment is a fairly easy solution, except when there is no longer space or money available for the equipment. The organization is then left with the option to either accept lower output, invest in more space at some cost, find additional funding, or focus on the output capabilities of the equipment.

The capability of the equipment will be somewhat limited by physics. A machine is basically only capable of performing so quickly. A car designed to have a top speed of 80 mph will have a difficult time going 150 mph under normal circumstances. Getting performance increases well beyond the norm is a difficult outcome to accomplish.

The next option that exists is to replace existing equipment with newer equipment that has higher operational capacity or enhanced operations-space capabilities. Smaller equipment rated at a lower capacity may free up space for additional machines to be purchased. Larger, faster equipment can allow for increased operations-space capacity, as well.

The first two options, therefore, are to either increase the total space that is available or to use the existing space more effectively. Of course, another option that exists is to maintain the current capacity and output capabilities of the organization and maintain existing financial performance.

Labor Output

Labor utilization is a crucial type of capacity to manage. Labor is a large component of an organization's costs. As with space and with other types of capacity, the organization must understand first what the expected demand of work will be, whether work means the number of

IN THE REAL WORLD

Planning For Productivity

Planning space is more than an activity to manage costs. According to space expert Jacqueline C. Vischer, effectively designing space and the accommodations within can not only reduce occupancy costs but might also increase worker effectiveness. As the organization seeks to reduce costs through space capacity reduction, it should also take the opportunity to strategically design the work tasks into the space, so that worker efficiency and effectiveness are increased.

shipments that are made by a department, the number of lawns that must be cut, or the number of hot air balloon rides that must be provided over a period. The demand or expected demand should be the basis for both desired capacity levels and anticipated changes to capacity levels.

With labor utilization, there are certain issues that must be effectively managed. One must manage the time that is worked and the amount of work that can be done during that time (see Equation 3.10).

$$\text{labor output} = \frac{\text{operations}}{\text{time}} \times \text{time} \qquad \textit{3.10}$$

Time

As described previously, time is impacted by people and how they manage their work or how they are managed. An organization cannot expect a person to work 24 hours each day for 7 days per week. There are natural limitations that ultimately limit the time that an individual can make available to the organization. Clearly, one-way organizations manage this constraint is to create the equivalent of a person who works 24 hours per day by creating multiple shifts. Three 8-hour shifts or two 12-hour shifts handle the single-person limitation very well.

Even if the people are physically present for work, it does not mean that all of the time is available for the work that they must perform. For a person who is physically at work for 10 hours, other activities such as meals, biological breaks, conversations, and just general downtime will keep them from being productive for the full 10 hours. In other cases, there may not be demand for the person to work at all. The net result is that, even though the person is at work, it is likely that the total time available or worked is less than the time in which he or she is physically present. Sometimes the organization can do something about the fact that they do not get 10 hours of work from each employee, sometimes they cannot. Sometimes the issue fixes itself, as employees choose to work more hours to make up for the time spent away from productive work.

The ultimate objective with managing work and time should be to get as close to full availability as possible without negatively impacting the quality of the life at work. Oftentimes, demand can increase availability. When people have a lot of work to do, they are more likely to do more work in the time available. Not increasing availability or allowing low-availability values can have a fairly large impact on the organization. A group of 10 people who are 80% available need two extra people to get the same number of hours of work as 8 people who are 100% available (see Equation 3.11).

$$64 \text{ hours} = 10 \text{ people} \times \frac{8 \text{ hours}}{\text{shift}} \times 80\%$$

$$64 = 8 \text{ people} \times \frac{8 \text{ hours}}{\text{shift}} \times 100\%$$

3.11

Increasing availability increases the number of management degrees of freedom available. With the increased availability comes either more work or the ability to reduce the amount of labor capacity.

$$72 \text{ hours} = 10 \text{ people} \times \frac{8 \text{ hours}}{\text{shift}} \times 90\%$$

$$72 = 9 \text{ people} \times \frac{8 \text{ hours}}{\text{shift}} \times 100\%$$

3.12

By increasing the availability by 10 percentage points, the organization gets either 72 hours of work or it can now reduce the total number of people by 1 (see Equation 3.12).

There is another component to managing availability. There is value-added work and non–value-added work that can be performed. Work that adds value is defined specifically by each organization, given the type of work that it does. Work that does not add value reduces the availability of an organization's labor capacity. Consider, for instance, the sales person who spends 20% of her time doing paperwork. Instead of selling for 40 hours, she only has 32 hours to sell because 8 hours are spent doing paperwork that may not be adding value to the selling process. Reducing her time spent on non–value-adding activities from 20% to 10% results in an increase in hours to 36. It is important to note that this productivity increase does not lead to cost savings. She is still paid the same salary, not considering commissions. Instead, it leads to increased capacity to sell. This increased ability to sell can ultimately lead to revenue enhancements.

The other option for increasing labor output is to focus on operations per unit time. Operations per unit time is largely a function of the competence and capability of the individual. From a competence perspective, a person who is more experienced in doing a job is likely to be faster at performing the job. This is reflected in ideas such as the learning curve, which suggests that the time required to perform an activity decreases at a relatively constant rate as volume or experience increases. Capability in this case reflects the overall ability of the person to perform a job. Some people are just better suited for a job than others. This may result in two individuals having different learning rates (see Exhibit 3.4) or people with the same learning rates but differing overall output levels (see Exhibit 3.5).

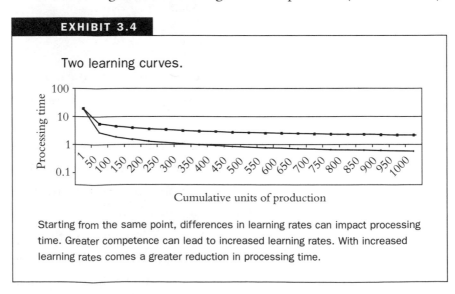

EXHIBIT 3.4

Two learning curves.

Starting from the same point, differences in learning rates can impact processing time. Greater competence can lead to increased learning rates. With increased learning rates comes a greater reduction in processing time.

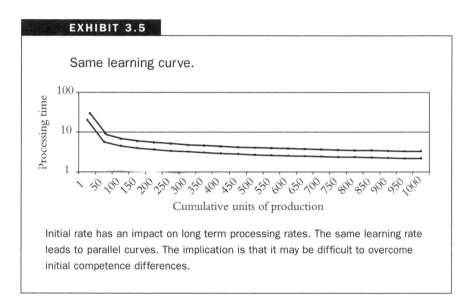

EXHIBIT 3.5

Same learning curve.

Initial rate has an impact on long term processing rates. The same learning rate leads to parallel curves. The implication is that it may be difficult to overcome initial competence differences.

There are a significant number of ways that people can impact competence and capability, from education and on-the-job training to the application of the best practices. Ultimately, organizations need to understand the extent to which capacity must be increased and plan to achieve that level of competence. Overall, benefits can be achieved by working on both availability and output rate. As suggested previously, organizations can increase their capacity to perform value-adding work by increasing availability, but by increasing capability and competence, more work can be done in a given period of time with the same input level.

Equipment Capacity

Equipment capacity, like labor capacity, is impacted by the output capabilities of the equipment and its availability (see Equation 3.13). The values in the equation are impacted by different issues, however.

$$\text{output in products} = \frac{\text{operations}}{\text{time}} \times \frac{\text{products}}{\text{operations}} \times \text{time} \times \text{utilization} \quad \textit{3.13}$$

Time

The time that a piece of equipment is available is impacted by its uptime capabilities and the availability of labor to operate the equipment. From an uptime perspective, the reliability of the equipment and the ability to repair the equipment can impact available time. Equipment that breaks down fairly frequently or that has a fairly lengthy mean-time-to-repair (MTTR) will have lower availability, all things being equal. This is one reason why preventive and predictive maintenance programs work so effectively. They focus on increasing the availability or uptime of machines. If it takes 1 less hour to repair a machine, that is 1 more hour that it can be available for productive work.

Labor availability is important, when labor is required to run the equipment. If a person is required to load and unload equipment, for example, the equipment is essentially only available when the labor is available to perform work. So, if the organization operates only one shift, the equipment is essentially only available for one shift. Some organizations have created automated operating environments: the so-called *lightless* factory that can operate in the dark 24 hours per day. Clearly, in an environment like this, labor is less of a constraint for machine availability.

Utilization

The utilization of equipment is often tied to the scheduling of the equipment, material availability, and set-up. Lack of utilization may not necessarily be a bad thing, as will be discussed in Chapters 5 and 7. However, lack of utilization at the wrong time may lead to limits in the organization's ability to create output. This will be discussed in detail in Chapter 5. Scheduled downtime results for multiple reasons, including lack of demand. Organizations might choose to reduce the number of products that are being created at a particular operation because it does not add to the organization's financial or operational performance. An operation producing products for which there is no demand might consume unneeded materials or slow down the operations within a process, leading to reduced cash and reduced throughput, respectively.

"Utilization" may mean different things to different organizations, but it is essentially the same concept applied differently. For a consulting firm, utilization might reflect billable hours. For a factory, utilization might reflect the time that a machine is operational. For an accounting department, it might reflect the time involved in processing invoices. When using utilization as a measure, it is important to explicitly define the value-added work, which is the numerator of the utilization equation (see Equation 3.14). One can argue that the value will always equal one because available time is spent working. Although this may be true in some cases, to get useful information from the ratio, one must be more specific about the numbers. The numerator should reflect work that is, again, adding value. Hence, a machine consuming unneeded labor and material capacity in the name of utilization should not be considered to be fully utilized because its work is artificial.

$$\text{utilization} = \frac{\textbf{value-added hours worked}}{\textbf{hours available}} \qquad 3.14$$

Material availability might be an issue, as equipment may be shut down when the operation has nothing to process. Operations in this position are left to be unutilized, which may or may not be positive for the organization, depending on the demand in the market for the products.

Standard Output

Operations-time measures and product–operations measures have been discussed throughout this chapter. When operations-time measures are combined with product–operations measures, the net results is an output measure, products–time (see Equation 3.15).

$$\frac{\text{products}}{\text{time}} = \frac{\text{products}}{\text{operation}} \times \frac{\text{operation}}{\text{time}} \qquad \textit{3.15}$$

Although the average values of each variable are often known, for various reasons, they will have standard deviations of varying magnitudes created by numerous influencing factors. This is where operations standards and labor standards might be useful by setting expectations for their capacity. For operations, financial, and planning purposes, the labor standards set expectations of what is possible.

The standard output measure is determined by looking at what work must be performed (methods) and the time required to perform the operation. Engineers and process specialists often work to understand and improve both measures, which can lead to additional capacity for producing value-added work. The standard can be used in this capacity as a benchmark measure for output. It is not necessary for the operations to always try to meet or exceed standards. This concept is discussed further in Chapters 5 and 7. The key criterion is to understand the standard and what it represents, so that it can be used for capacity planning and communications.

Utilization, time, and product output are the important measures to consider when considering equipment output. Organizations must comprehend the demand being placed on the resource, so that it can manage these three components effectively. As discussed in Chapter 5, managers must have flexibility as they manage equipment capacity. Improperly utilizing equipment can have a strong negative influence on operations and financials. For example, just because an expensive piece of equipment exists and costs the organization money is no reason to run the equipment unnecessarily or excessively. Such decisions can increase costs, disrupt flow, and increase process leadtime.

IT Output

IT output is similar to equipment output, except for the fact that IT capacity may not be limited to the availability of labor resources. With many IT systems, there is an option to schedule and run long, or special jobs during times when there is little or no labor using or operating the equipment. The benefit, of course, is that lead times are not impacted by jobs requiring a large amount of the system's capacity.

Capacity concepts apply to both computing systems and to the networks on which they run. The computing systems have storage capacity and processing capacity. The network has capacity to pass data from one location to another. Rather than going into the details of the architecture behind both components of IT capacity, IT capacity will be viewed at a macro level by considering how to measure its ability to provide the desired information and data. There are a number of resources available in both the Internet and in book form that can support the reader seeking greater detail regarding specific architecture-based capacity management.

As with other types of equipment, organizations must understand the demand that is placed on its computing resources. Improperly sizing computing capacity or network capacity creates notable difficulties. The reason, simply, is that even if the IT capacity is operating at its maximum levels, it gives the appearance of being slow, when inundated with demand. If one person submits a program to run on a computer while the computer is available, he or she might enjoy a reasonable response time. However, as the demand on the computer increases, the "time-in-system" for the program increases. Time-in-system reflects on overall lead time measure that can vary depending on the work load. Simply, more work often leads to increased wait time, which increases the time from request submitted to receipt of response. The rate of processing time and output may be the same, but they are perceived to be slower than the individual because of its wait time.

Because IT capacity often provides support for the other types of capacity, the focus in this book will be in how it impacts the other capacity and, ultimately, the organization's ability to perform its job. Considering the output equation, organizations must manage their IT resource capacity similarly to how they would manage equipment capacity but with a bit more freedom (see Equation 3.16).

$$\text{output (information)} = \frac{\text{operations}}{\text{time}} \times \frac{\text{information}}{\text{operations}} \times \text{time} \qquad 3.16$$

If the capability of IT capacity is measured as the product of these components, assuming that availability and utilization are not issues at the moment, the organization must manage the three to achieve the desired output. Time is a given. One can choose an arbitrary time period, and if the computing resources are to be available, they basically can be made available. Operations per unit time are limited by the design of the hardware. The speed of the processes and the ability to send and receive data will limit what can be done per second, for example. To increase the output, therefore, one should either purchase faster equipment, upgrade existing equipment to the extent that the previous bottleneck was relieved, or write programs that use the equipment more effectively. Vector programs written specifically for vector computers are an example of how this can be done. When a vector program is run on a vector processor, it takes full advantage of the architecture of the vector computer and, therefore, runs much faster than if it were to run on a scalar processor.

Material Output

The final type of output to be considered is material output. As with all other utilization, it is tied to how capably the organization can utilize the materials. Output is also a function of the amount of materials that are available. Material capacity is binary, in that there are either enough materials available to support the desired level of production or there are not. If the materials exist, there will be no impact on machine utilization unless, or course, poor process management creates problems. Without the required amount of materials, equipment utilization can be lowered.

To determine product output, one must consider how the product is made from the materials. A car will likely use four or five tires and one windshield. The bill of materials will describe how much of which materials will be required. The theoretical numbers in the bill of materials are not enough, however. Many times, waste created by processes suggests that more pieces of certain components might be required because some of the materials are lost as a result of the process. This could lead to the fact that, when assessing total material capacity as it relates to product output, another component must be considered: a loss factor of some sort, or a yield rate. Equation 3.17 represents the equation that one can use to define material capacity in terms of products.

$$\textbf{products} = \frac{\textbf{products}}{\textbf{materials}} \times \textbf{materials} \times \textbf{yield rate} \qquad 3.17$$

The components of this equation are very straightforward. Product-materials represents how many products can be manufactured from a base of materials. Four tires (materials) are required to make one car (product). These ratios are determined when the products are initially designed. The yield rate represents what percentage of the initial materials end up in finished products. So, if 98% of all tires end up on a car and if 100 tires are in inventory, only 24 cars can be made (Equation 3.18).

$$24 \text{ cars} = \frac{1 \text{ car}}{4 \text{ tires}} \times 100 \text{ tires} \times 0.98 \qquad \textit{3.18}$$

Two tires will remain afterward. If the organization needs to make 25 cars, it must buy more than 100 tires to compensate. In this case, the organization might need to have 103 tires in inventory to make 25 cars. The quantity of 103 units is determined by manipulating Equation 3.15, resulting in Equation 3.19. The decimals are included here to show that 102 tires may not be enough. Since one cannot buy 0.04 tires, the organization might work to choose 103 tires rather than 102 tires.

$$\text{materials} = \text{products} \times \frac{\text{materials}}{\text{products}} \times \frac{1}{\text{yield rate}}$$
$$= 25 \text{ cars} \times \frac{4 \text{ tires}}{1 \text{ car}} \times \frac{1}{0.98} \qquad \textit{3.19}$$
$$= 102.04 \text{ tires or } 103 \text{ tires}$$

Summary

The purpose of this chapter was to introduce the basic measures of capacity. We focused mostly on time, space, products, and tasks. We then began to combine them to create measures that can be used everyday to measure capacity and capacity output. The next chapters will begin to use this information to create and manage processes and to provide a basis for understanding the financial dynamics that result. Chapter 4 will focus on creating processes and the information needed, so that the right capacity levels can be determined. Chapter 5 talks about the processes themselves. Processes are created by combining entities and operations. Chapter 6 discusses how capacity impacts important financial measures. Chapter 7 will bring all of the topics together to help organizations manage toward optimizing their operations.

Endnotes

[1] "Area" will be used for the rest of the book, but the discussions can be expanded easily to volume in three-dimensional space.

[2] This problem is only being considered from an operational perspective at this point.

CHAPTER 4

Process Fundamentals

After reading this chapter, you will be able to:

- Define a process from a capacity perspective
- Understand what questions need to be addressed when creating a process

Introduction

To this point, the text has focused on discussing the importance of capacity, the types of capacity, and fundamental ways to measure capacity. Capacity, as discussed in Chapter 1, is a significant component of an organization's costs and assets. Chapter 2 focused on introducing the five types of capacity referred to as *capacity entities* and discussing their importance in the organization. These included the space, labor, equipment, information technology, and materials, each of which is often used on a daily basis within the organization. Entities are the most basic capacity components within an organization. Entities are combined to create operations, which were discussed in Chapter 3. Chapter 3 began to combine capacity types into operations and defined the types of measures that resulted. The chapter also focused on the base capacity measurement components—time, space, operations, and products—that are the building blocks used to measure capacity at fundamental and more advanced levels.

This chapter will build on this foundation to create the first aspect of understanding how capacity, in the form of entities and operations, will come together to create processes. *A process is the set of tasks or operations that create some type of desirable output.* The output can exist in multiple forms, including, but not limited to, being a product, a service, a plan, or an action. Processes can range from product development to manufacturing to delivering consulting services to accounts payable and practically everything in between. This chapter will focus on the parameters that surround the process itself. The parameters surrounding the process are very important because the parameters—the *how*, the *why*, the *when*, and the *where*—influence how we design, manage, and measure the processes. This, in turn, dictates how the capacity should be managed. Rather than going directly into measures and managing processes, therefore, this chapter will introduce fundamental concepts that the manager should understand and keep in mind when designing and managing processes and the associated capacity.

Since practically everything that an organization does is either formally or informally tied to some type of a process, to achieve desirable financial and operational performance, the processes must operate efficiently and effectively. For efficient and effective processes, the capacity components that make up the process and the management thereof must ensure that each component is contributing in ways that enhance the operating parameters of the process. The operating parameters include the desired input coupled with the desired output of the process. The desired input includes the right amount of input capacity, such as materials and labor. The desired output includes having the finished product at the right time, the right cost, and the right quality levels.

To ensure efficient and effective operations, the measures used to manage the process must begin with the process itself and must lead to designing operational measures that support the objectives of the process. Measures for operations that do not support the objectives of the process should be eliminated. However, organizations often focus their measures not on the process but on the operations. Focusing on the operation rather than on the process can help optimize the operation to the peril of the process.[1] Such a management approach will lead to undesirable operational and financial performance. As discussed to varying degrees in the next four chapters, the emphasis must be placed on ensuring that processes can operate as designed, so that they can provide the necessary output for the organization.

This chapter will begin with defining *processes*. Entities and operations come together and interact, so that processes can be created. As the operators come together, the concept of interactions becomes important because many process inefficiencies occur as a result of the inefficiencies created by the interactions. Hand-offs, for instance, can be poorly designed or may encourage mistakes. This leads to long wait times, the need to rework the work product, and the need to carry excess capacity. What the process and its interactions are capable of should be dictated by the purpose of the process, what it makes, for whom, and how. That is the essence of this chapter. Chapter 5 and beyond will provide the detail necessary to understand and manage processes with greater accuracy.

Process Creation and Management

The first issue that an organization must consider when thinking about processes is output. There are many components to output that should be defined prior to determining how to create the product. For the purpose of simplicity, *product* will be used from here onward to reflect the output of a process. The second issue to consider is how to assemble

Case for Simple and Effective Processes

The authors of *Simplicity Wins: How Germany's Mid-Sized Industrial Companies Succeed* believe that simple structures, processes, and lead to competitive advantages for the companies that they studied. The importance of the process design being as simple as possible to support business objectives is a salient point throughout their book. In it, they identified a number of levers that the companies used to gain advantages:

- *Product range and customer structure:* concentrate on volume segments, and core customers and core products offering optimal customer value.

- *Vertical integration:* capitalize on areas where the company is strong, by expanding vertical integration; otherwise, when out-sourcing, reduce number of suppliers and integrate them better.

- *Development:* increase downstream development efficiency by reducing risk upstream, and innovate in small rapid steps.

- *Location structure and logistics:* configure locations around products—in dedicated plants or "plants within plants"—and optimize materials flow.

- *Technology:* simplify engineering before automating.

- *Organization:* ensure transparent, simplified, decentralized structures, and create entrepreneurial spirit.

the various types of *capacity*. The capacity can be assembled or may exist in one of three ways:

1. *Use an existing process.* For organizations that need to manage their current capacity more effectively or that have operations with adequate capacity and competence, they may look to an existing process as a basis.

2. *Modify an existing process.* If the current process does not work as effectively as it should, organizations may look to improve the existing process to achieve desired results.

3. *Design a new process.* When the existing process does not exist, or if the current process is incapable of achieving the required objectives, one may need to design a new process.

As a third issue, the right *measures and management approaches* must be in place, so that the organization can manage the processes effectively. To get the most out of a process, the organization must understand how various types of capacity interact, so that the interactions themselves and the results of the interactions can be managed effectively.

Start with the Product in Mind

The initial step in creating a process is to start with the product in mind. What is it that the process is going to create? When trying to understand the product, one should ask the following questions:

- What are we creating?
- Why are we creating this product, and for whom is it being made?
- When should we make the product?

What Is It That We Will Be Creating?

The purpose of this question is to build the foundation necessary to effectively define what the product of the process will be. One must understand the nature of the product. Is it a physical product, an intellectual product, or an emotional product? One must also understand the components of success that the product will impact. When creating the product, is the purpose to manage or reduce costs, increase revenues, improve working capital, or improve customer satisfaction? Are there other, less tangible benefits that are being sought?

Finally, one must understand how the process will interact with its user base. Will the process need to interact with other firms or locations as it makes its products? Must the final product be in a specific location that will ultimately require flexibility in the process and its planning?

What Is the Type of Product Being Made?

Is the product a physical item, such as one that will come out of an assembly line process? With physical products, the process must support the interactions of possibly all five capacity entities. There is space capacity that is utilized by equipment and labor that is processing materials. The effective planning and management of the entities will likely involve IT capacity to provide the necessary information for planning purposes. If the product is an intellectual product or program, such as a strategy for an organization or an education program, you must understand the capacity requirements here, as well. Clearly, labor is involved. Additionally, IT capacity will likely be used, and space capacity might be an issue, as well.

What Are the Components of Success?

When considering the design and development of the product, you must also understand the components of success for the product. This is a very important point because certain components of the process will be emphasized over others, depending on the purpose of the product internally or how the product is being positioned in the market. For internal processes that are not market-facing, speed and efficiency are often the components of success. The organization should seek to provide as much output as possible with as little input as is reasonably possible. For market-facing products, if the product is positioned in the market as a low-cost product, the process must be designed to achieve the desired throughput with as little capacity as possible. If the objective is revenue enhancement, the process has to be as fast and as flexible as possible. If the organization seeks working-capital reduction, the process must be able to operate with minimum inventory and must be fast, so that it reduces the overall time that the organization has its cash tied up. If customer satisfaction is the objective, fast access to information and quick decisions are prerequisites. Because other components of success exist, the organization must clearly understand what they are, what weight they carry, and how to manage the capacity to achieve the components of success.

External Interactions

Finally, organizations must understand what interactions the product might have with external sources. Must the product, for instance, interact with other firms for processing or approvals? Must the final product end up in specific locations, which would decide where space capacity would be utilized, how it is managed, and how the interactions are managed?

Understanding the product itself (physical or not), the components of success, and how the product will interact with other organizations is very important when defining the *what* of the product; however, it is not enough. After the *what* has been identified, one must now shift to the *why*.

Why Are We Creating This Product?

The *why* of the product is critical for process design. The product must satisfy some strategic or tactical criterion of the organization, and understanding the *why* will help make the reason more salient. When focusing on the *why*, there are a number of questions that can be posed. These questions can address, but not be limited to, issues such as:

- Is the product tied to an organizational strategy or is it tactically focused?
- Is it a one-time product or is it reusable?
- Are the needs specific or broad? High volume or low?

To help with the questioning process, each of these questions will be examined in a bit of detail.

Products Tied to Organization Strategy? Tactically Focused?

These questions help organizations understand how the process should be positioned. If the solution is tied to organizational strategy, the outcome of the process might be different than if it is tactically focused. If the product and, therefore, the process are strategically focused, the organization might want to improve its capabilities over time rather than expect a major impact with one stroke. Strategically focused processes will likely be designed to be good and improved over time, using continuous improvement types of techniques. Such an improvement strategy creates a knowledge base that is difficult to duplicate, even if the organization explains its approach to competitors. Not having lived the challenges and not having overcome them, the observer will not likely have the competence to compete, even if it copied the processes in much detail.

Tactically focused products and processes, however, tend to focus on a quick fix. These fixes often involve reengineered processes and/or the application of best practices. Such actions involve completely redesigning a process to achieve drastic short-term improvement. When a process is redesigned to a significant extent, organizations often do so because there is a critical need, such as a broken process that is causing the organization to have operational difficulty. Application of best practices, too, is more of a tactical move than a strategic move. Best practices are often created as a result of some operational context that requires their existence. However, organizations tend to try to implement best practices without the complete context of what created them and why they were successful in the first place.

Just-in-time, for example, created a number of what could have been considered best or leading practices, such as the pull system for inventory management, small batch-sized operations, and quick changeover. Any one of the practices on its own was considered a best practice, but organizations often applied them out of context or without full context. The result was multiple failed implementations of small-batch production or pull-inventory management. That which necessitated the approach may not have existed within the organization, leading to a lack of importance and competence tied to the process. Another failure is one of misunderstanding how practices must interact with each other. Many organizations tried small-batch production and pull-based scheduling techniques without the proper quality controls and short changeover capabilities.

Finally, the other danger of best practice implementation is that if everyone implements the same best practices, there is a risk of competence convergence, suggesting that everyone is capable of doing the same thing. For tactical products or processes, this might be acceptable. Strategically, it might not be.

The organization must determine, therefore, how the product and process will improve the organization. If the issue is strategy, the approach will be one of slower, steadier improvement and competence development; tactically, organizations will follow the lead of others for quick improvement. Reengineering processes often involves completely redesigning or redeveloping processes. Although reengineering can be used to gain a strategic advantage, organizations that need such improvement tend to reengineer in times of some difficulty. Organizations with poorly performing operating processes may seek to reengineer as a way to create an immediate impact.

Is the Product a One-Time Product or Is It Repeatable?

Whether the product is going to be created only once or repeated multiple times has a major impact on the design and capabilities of the process itself. Processes designed to create a one-time product, such as a legal defense or a specialized manufactured product, require different capabilities and competencies than processes that create and sell repeatable products, such as cars (see Exhibit 4.1).

One-Time Products   Products that are made one time have very different process requirements than those that are repeatable. One-time products require processes that are very flexible in their competence because they must be able to be utilized by multiple products over the long term. Therefore, if only one unit of a product is going to be produced, the capacity must be able to produce other types of products to make up its available time. From a quality perspective, therefore, competence must be designed into the task itself because interactions between operations or entities might be unique. This

---

EXHIBIT 4.1

Approach to improving quality, cost, and lead time or cycle time varies based on whether the process creates one-time or repeatable processes.

	One Time Products	**Repeatable**
Quality	Designed into tasks	Designed into process
Cost	Typically higher competence and capacity	Lower and more predictable
Time	Slower and more complicated	Much faster

TIPS & TECHNIQUES

Organizations that are averse to a process-oriented way of thinking oftentimes inadvertently create one-time products. If processes involving people working together to achieve a common goal do not exist, you are likely to carry far more capacity than necessary, which can clearly impact your profitability and cash flow.

limits the ability to improve quality by managing interactions. From a cost perspective, the one-time product requires, on the average, resources that are highly competent. Automation and task break-downs that yield certain operational efficiencies are often not an option. What is required are highly skilled workers who are capable of handling varying types of work with great competence. From a time perspective, one-time products will likely take longer because the organization is often not as capable of handling processes that are nonrepeating. Competence regarding how to plan and manage the steps of the process and the interactions will not have a chance to be created and incorporated into the process to result in time improvements, such as those described in the learning curve section in Chapter 6.

For repeatable products, the necessary competencies are often easier to create. Processes are broken down into repeatable steps, such as that which occurred with the redesign of manufacturing processes in the Ford era and post–Ford era. What was learned from Ford and Frederick Taylor, the father of industrial engineering, was that a repeatable process can be broken down into repeatable operations or tasks. When this is the case, a person may be required to learn a repeatable task rather than how to flexibly operate a machine by performing multiple tasks. This increases the relative ease with which one can prepare someone for a job but limits what the person is capable of doing. Quality, therefore, is designed into the process, so that anyone who has been trained to do the job can deliver a high-quality product. From a cost perspective, the simplicity of operations leads to operations with lower-skilled resources required and fewer mistakes being made on average. From a time perspective, the relative simplicity associated with planning and managing repeatable processes creates clear advantages. The routing of the work product and repeatable steps create the potential for a fast-moving product environment.

It should be clear, then, that the approach to process design and the relevant competencies should be tied to the type of product and its volume or frequency. Processes supporting one-time products require different competencies than those for repeatable products. This will impact decisions leading to the capability and competence of the capacity.

Finally, one must determine whether the product is to meet a specific need or a broad need. Processes that create products for a very specific and unique purpose must have the needs of the purpose designed into the process. The processes used to design and develop Formula 1 cars, for instance, are very different from those used for a general automobile. The Formula 1 processes must be more precise and must reflect the demands of a vehicle whose engine turns 18,000 RPM and can create 3 to 4 g's of braking force. The process must be much more aligned with the needs of the user of the product. In contrast, the processes used to develop a general-purpose automobile will be tied to the needs of the user to a much lesser degree. A Dodge Neon has drivers who range from the proverbial little old lady from Pasadena to weekend racers. The process must reflect the need to make a high-quality vehicle in large numbers and one that is used for various purposes. The objective with the Neon, therefore, is to emphasize volume and quality, so that the price of buying and maintaining the vehicle will remain reasonable. Hence, when considering the design of the process and the relevant capabilities, the nature of the product's use will play a significant role in consider-ing the capabilities and competence of the process.

The next question that must be considered from a process design perspective is, for whom is the product being made? This question should be considered for more reasons than are initially obvious. First, recall that "the product" can be anything from a piece of information to a strategy to a check to a manufactured product. The product will often be used by someone else as an input to their knowledge base, their work, or their lifestyle. Therefore, it is very important to reflect the need of the recipient of the product in the process itself. Required in this knowledge is, *who* will use the product, *how* they are going to use the product, and *why* they are going to use the product to obtain what is necessary.

Who Is Going to Use the Product?

The *who* reflects the need to address issues such as location, and the framing of *how* they would use the product at a high level. There are two categories of probable users:

- Those who give to us
- Those who take from us

For those who give to us, there is often a process associated with acknowledging receipt, providing future demand information, and paying for what has been received. There are processes that can be defined for each of these activities. There are also processes that focus on seeking those from whom we would like to take and the process of taking. This can include seeking competitive information from research sources, just as it can include the procurement of parts to manufacture a product. Each is a process that requires effective design and capacity utilization.

For those who take from us, there are two perspectives to consider. The first reflects the fact that some will take from us in an open-loop fashion. "Open loop" here refers to the fact that once the transaction occurs, interactions between groups happen seldom if at all. The second perspective is that of an ongoing interaction between the provider and the taker. Both are very important from process design and capacity management perspectives. From a process design perspective, considering the former, there might be a number of "one-ofs" that make it difficult to plan the capacity. Without a constant, predictable source of demand, how will one understand and, therefore, plan the amount of capacity required? There might not be an effective feedback mechanism that provides the demand data back into the process, nor might it provide useful process improvement recommendations. For the latter, the organization will work to seek as much feedback as possible to aid in the planning of the capacity. Additionally, since there are significant interactions with this group (takers), it is easier to design specific processes that aid in the efficiency of both participants. Because the transactions occur regularly, it makes sense for the organization to seek as many efficiencies as possible. An automotive company may not want to set up electronic data interchange transactions for a person buying a car, for instance, but may work to set them up with those who buy their parts in significant quantities on a regular basis.

It is important to note that the above discussion is as applicable for internal customers and suppliers as it is for external customers and suppliers. In fact, from a financial perspective, it might be more important. As will be discussed in the process design and capacity optimization section, process efficiency leads to the ability to provide more output or reduce the amount of capacity required for the same output. In either case, the benefit can be positive for the organization.

Timing of the Solution: When Do We Make It?

When one considers the *when* of the product, it has a significant impact on identifying, creating, and managing capacity. The extent to which there is an impact is determined by the context supporting how *when* is being used. *When* can be now, reflecting immediacy and suggesting the timing of delivery in a short timeframe. Should it be made available over the next few hours or days? *When* can also be a long-term focus on issues such as rolling out new products and determining the future capacity requirements of doing so.

The short-term *when* focuses on the details of scheduling operations to get the most from the processes. The interaction of the operations is critical in determining the time implications of decision-making. As discussed in each of the last four chapters of the book, how one manages and schedules processes is as important as the physical capability of the operations that make up the process itself. Improperly scheduling processes can lead to poor utilization of the resources and extended lead times. Although the processing time for each unit might remain the same, the overall time spent waiting to be processed is ultimately offset by the apparent benefit of fast processing capabilities because poor scheduling can create large queues.

From a long-term perspective, one must focus on the capacity of the existing and/or future systems. Future planning involves trying to determine the demand at some point in the future and translate that into capacity requirements. The anticipated demand requirements can be translated into either capacity growth or reduction requirements for the organization. Is there enough labor to meet expected demand over time? Is there enough space, equipment, and materials to meet the expected demand? The decisions are much more strategic in nature and involve a potential resizing of the organization to ensure desired operational and financial performance.

More time will be spent on the *why* of delivering products in Chapters 5 and 7. The *when*, as found later in chapters, has a major impact on how the organization needs to manage its capacity from both tactical and long-term perspectives. It will, then, influence the amount of space, labor, equipment, IT, and materials you ultimately need for optimal performance.

Where Does the Product Need to Be?

The *where* with capacity involves trying to determine what capacity needs to be in what location to meet either current or future demand. This is very important in certain industries or markets, where being close to the recipient is an important criterion to meeting business objectives. Examples of such industries or markets would be products or services the effective and efficient delivery of which would be tied to geography. An example of location not being important is the creation of web sites that focus on information delivery. One might go to the web site, where the creation and storage of information is, but it happens to be of no consequence to the one seeking the product. The key issue is to ensure that the product is in the place necessary for further action, when desired.

The *where* involves tying the products to where demand requires them to be. If there are geographic issues that need to be considered, they are factored into the ultimate solution. Amazon.com does not need to have a presence in every city to meet its desired customer service levels.

Summary

By asking these questions about processes, you have a complete picture of the operating parameters of the process. You understand what is being made, why, for whom, where, and when. You understand whether the process has strategic or tactical importance. You know what the critical components of success are. Chapter 5 picks up from here and begins to define processes. The chapter also introduces the criteria involved in measuring the process and will itself be the foundation for the Chapter 6 discussion on financial dynamics and the Chapter 7 discussion on optimization.

Endnotes

[1] See for example, Eliyahu Goldratt and Jeff Cox, *The Goal: A Process of Ongoing Improvement*, Revised Edition (Croton-on-Hudson, N.Y.: North River Press, 1986).

CHAPTER 5

Creating Processes from Capacity Entities and Operations

After reading this chapter, you will be able to:

- Understand the fundamental types of processes
- Understand how operations interact
- Understand key operation and process measures
- Begin to understand constraints and how they influence the capacity and capabilities of a process

Introduction

To this point in the book, the focus has been on introducing the various capacity components. The book started with an explanation of why capacity management was important. The key point to take away from that discussion is the idea that capacity represents and significantly influences an organization's profits, assets, and working capital. In Chapter 1, we began to understand the *why* and the *how* behind the relationships between capacity and the firm's profits, assets, and working capital. In Chapter 2, the focus was on introducing the various types of capacity and the fundamental measures. This was an important chapter for two reasons. First, we began to look at capacity in a different light. Whereas before, capacity represented space and many times equipment, and IT, and sometimes labor but usually not materials, we now look at capacity as not only including these components in their entirety but also the interactions between these components. The interactions between the capacity components created operations. Interactions between operations, for the purposes of delivering a product or a service, create processes. Chapter 4 focused on the essentials of defining the purpose of processes. What does the process create? For whom are the processes and products being created? How are they going to use the product? Where does the product need to be? This information should be used as context–setting for this chapter.

The purpose of this chapter is to bring together the information from the first four chapters to create an understanding of how the processes create their respective products and what the key measures or indicators are.[1] The chapter introduces four types of generic processes and discusses each, providing information such as:

- An introduction to the process type, including possible answers to the questions in Chapter 4
- A discussion about the various capacity components that are involved:
  - Entities
  - Operations
- A discussion about the interactions between capacity components
- Key measures for each capacity component

There are two things that the reader must keep in mind while reading through this chapter. First, every company performs these processes differently. It would be impossible to represent every nuance of an organization's processes in enough detail for it to be applied in detail for every process at every organization in existence. Rather, the point is for the reader to capture the concepts and the essential issues for the process, so that the concepts can be applied to the specifics of their organization. Second, costs and financial issues will be discussed in detail in the next chapter. Although they may be brought up to create or support context, the real details regarding how to measure capacity from a cost perspective will be discussed in Chapter 6.

The processes that will be considered in this chapter are:

- Conversion processes, where machines convert materials into a product. Examples might be manufacturing or food preparation.

- Organizational support processes that are the more traditional processes that exist within organizations and include processes, such as procurement, accounts receivables, hiring, and expense reporting.

- Design processes, where one takes ideas and converts them into a new concept. This can include product development or strategy development.

The list is not exhaustive. Again, the reader should begin to identify certain processes with what their attributes are and then to begin managing the process accordingly. Such a process will help reinforce the ideas and help the reader get out of the box created by this book, so that the concepts can be applied creatively to any operation.

The approach taken in this chapter is to begin with conversion processes. Much about processes in general occurs in conversion processes and, therefore, can be conveniently explained. After discussing conversion processes, the chapter will discuss any nuances that occur with the other two types of processes described in the book.

Conversion Processes

Conversion processes involve the use of equipment to convert materials into some sort of a product. Examples include manufacturing and certain types of food service industries, such as restaurants. The conversion itself focuses on taking materials and, through the use of equipment and

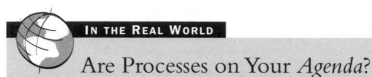

IN THE REAL WORLD

Are Processes on Your *Agenda*?

About processes, Michael Hammer says in *The Agenda*,

- Processes are what create the results that a company delivers to its customers. Value is created by the entire process, which consists of related activities (read: operations/tasks) working together toward a common goal.

- The activities that make up a process are related and organized. The process should be designed to have no non–value-adding activities and should be performed in an order that is not arbitrary.

- Each of the activities must work together for the achievement of a common goal.

- Processes are not ends-in-themselves. The purpose is to align that and those which make up the process with the common goal of delivering products (or services) to the customer.[a]

[a] Michael Hammer, *The Agenda* (New York: Crown Business, 2001).

sometimes labor, converting the materials into a useful product or service. Examples abound for manufacturing. There are cars, computers, and the equipment used to make equipment. Practically anything fabricated in a factory represents manufacturing as a process. There is also the textiles and garments industry, where everything from basic materials to the creation of clothing are processed. Clearly, manufacturing is a wide-ranging concept, and the ideas discussed in this section will apply to all manufacturing-related processes.

In the service industry, there are a significant number of examples. As a manufacturing process takes windows, doors, tires, and metal to assemble an automobile, a restaurant must take the various ingredients that exist and convert them into a desirable meal. There may be preparation before cooking, such as cleaning, cutting, sauce preparation, and other activities prior to the actual cooking process.

In these and other cases, the focus is on the concept of bringing all capacity components together to create the process. In the conversion process, you often find the use of at least four, and often five, of the capacity entities at work (see Exhibit 5.1). The only entity that may or may not be at work is information technology, and that should, and often does, reflect the value that IT adds to the process.

The *what* of conversion processes is simple. Conversion processes create physical products from other items. Therefore, the specific product is often easily defined: a chair, a plate of fried rice. Whatever the product, the objective of the process is to make the product in a manner that is focused on operational capabilities (quality, availability, or lead time), on financial desires (profitability and working capital), or some combination of both.

The *how* of conversion processes is where the difficulty arises. How does an organization take its capacity components and create the products while understanding the impact on issues such as quality, availability, profit, and working capital? The next few sections will answer this question while also addressing or bringing into context the other questions.

The *how* of the conversion process involves taking items, putting them into the process, and converting them from their original state to

---

EXHIBIT 5.1

Conversion processes tend to include all capacity entities.

Entities at work	Likelihood
Space	High
Labor	Medium-High
Equipment	High
IT	Low-High
Materials	High

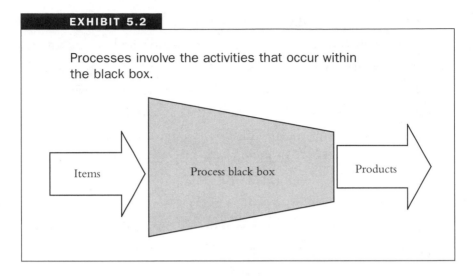

EXHIBIT 5.2

Processes involve the activities that occur within the black box.

Items → Process black box → Products

the final state. This final state serves as the product or the service, which is the output of the process (see Exhibit 5.2). The conversion process can range from one step to many steps, with each step being comprised of operations or tasks. An example might be the system found in Exhibit 5.3. In this exhibit, there are three operations:

- Primary conversion
- Secondary operations
- Assembly

Primary conversion might include activities such as taking a raw material and making it into a processable material. Iron ore requires conversion into a state that will be supported by the equipment that will process it. This allows for the rapid conversion into finished products. The same is true for wheat, which is processed into flour, and ultimately made into pasta. Secondary operations may involve various equipment-based operations, such as casting, forming, or machining in a manufacturing environment, and may involve cooking the pasta and other ingredients in a restaurant. The final step is assembly, which involves putting together the many components necessary to make the final product. The same holds true in a restaurant environment, where the many products are brought together to make the final dish. In each step, one can begin to analyze the capacity components that are involved.

Understanding the Dynamics of Operation Capacity

The dynamics of operation capacity reflect what is going on within an operation. It considers how the capacity entities will interact to perform the requisite tasks. The interactions create competencies that should be measured and managed. The next few sections will discuss some of the key aspects of understanding some of the dynamics of capacity and their influencing factors.

EXHIBIT 5.3

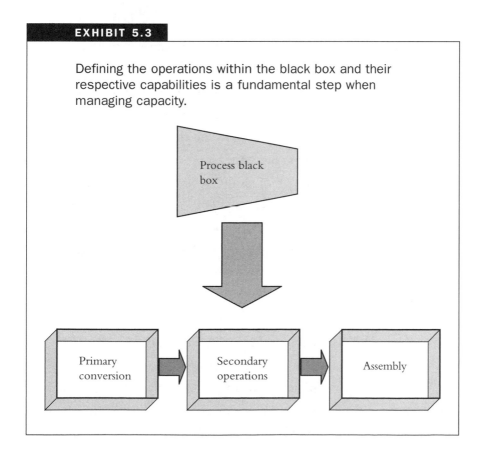

Defining the operations within the black box and their respective capabilities is a fundamental step when managing capacity.

TIPS & TECHNIQUES

- Capacity management should exist in the context of processes. The measurements used and the amount of capacity should be tied to the demand placed on the process.

- Your firm may want to appoint process owners or captains who are responsible for the operation of the process. The objective will be to have the owner manage the process, its resources, and the overall output of the process.

Materials

Materials are whatever is processed in the operation. For the primary operation, as an example, the material input might be raw materials that must be converted into metal in a manufacturable form. The maximum potential amount of manufactured material output is tied to the amount of raw material that is available and the capability of the operation. The same holds true in a restaurant where the amount of pasta is tied not only to the amount of flour and other ingredients that are available but also to the capability of the process. You get less pasta if 20% of the flour is lost in the operation than if only 10% is lost. For the second operation, the material input might be the material output from the first operation along with other materials that have been either purchased from the outside or produced internally. Similarly, the third operation will likely take material input from the second operation and other sources and assemble them into a final product.

Material availability can also impact equipment utilization when the material is available in limited quantities. Equipment that is starved for materials might find itself not being utilized to its maximum potential, even though it is available to be utilized. This may not be a bad situation, depending on the subsequent management action, as we will see later in this chapter and in Chapter 7, when the discussion will focus on process optimization. In fact, you may plan material shortages to force lower utilization of certain equipment. This translates into excess capacity that gives management multiple options for managing the capacity.

Equipment

The equipment used for the primary conversion has its own capacity, as well. As discussed in Chapters 2 and 3, the capacity of the equipment itself is tied to its own processing capability and availability. For many practical purposes, the machine determines the maximum output rate capability (units per hour or weight per hour), although, depending on the tasks at hand, it might be influenced by the competence of the operator. The availability of the equipment has natural components and organization-influenced components, as does the operational capacity of the equipment. Naturally, some machines are more reliable than others, leading to increased potential availability. Additionally, some machines are much more complicated in design and may require more time to repair if and when they go down, which may, of course, impacts availability.

Labor

Labor is often required to oversee operations and processes. With a fully manual operation, the operating and planning of the operation will require the full support of labor. Additionally, maintenance of the equipment, the tasks associated with operating the equipment, and ensuring the quality of the process and its output are labor intensive. In these cases, the *total availability* is 24 hours a day, although the *expected availability* is constrained to when the workers are available to operate the equipment. In the case of fully automatic operations, the equipment may be less reliant on labor for its availability. It must be repaired and maintained at times, but its total availability is limited only by the number of hours in a day.

Space

Space is the last capacity component that will be required for conversion processes. The materials, equipment, and labor will all take up space. Space may constrain the amount of equipment or type of equipment that can exist, can limit the amount of material capacity that can exist, and may also limit the amount of labor that can be involved in the process.

Creating Process Output

To create the process output, assume, simply, that there is a process where the first operation consumes raw materials and converts them into a form that is useable by the second process. The second process will create material output that is used by the third process in its assembly operations along with other materials. Assume that these other materials have been purchased from the outside. Each operation has its own theoretical output capacity determined by the product of the total availability and the output per unit time (Equation 5.1). Hence, with a 24-hour day, and at a rate of 5 units per hour, the theoretical output capacity of this operation is 120 units. It is important to understand this number. It represents what is theoretically possible if there was no equipment downtime and if the machine was operating during the full 24 hours of each day.

$$\frac{\text{theoretical output capacity}}{\text{day}} = \frac{\text{total availability (hours)}}{\text{day}} \times \frac{\text{unit}}{\text{hour}} \qquad 5.1$$

This is often an unrealistic expectation, however. Many factors, including operating shifts that do not cover a full 24-hour day, limit the availability of the machines. Therefore, to understand more closely the expectations of the operation, one would choose to use the *expected availability* as found in Equation 5.2.

$$\frac{\text{expected output capacity}}{\text{day}} = \frac{\text{expected availability (hours)}}{\text{day}} \times \frac{\text{unit}}{\text{hour}} \qquad 5.2$$

Using the same example, if the expected availability is 16 hours, representing two 8-hour shifts, the expected output capacity would only be 80 units. As shown in Exhibit 5.4, there is a direct relationship, defined by the output rate, which exists between the expected availability and the expected capacity of the operation.

Finally, the utilization of the equipment impacts the *realized* capacity. The utilization represents the percentage of time that equipment is operational over its available hours. So, if a piece of equipment is available for 16 hours and is only utilized at 50% operating at full rate, the realized output is 40 units, although the expected capacity would be 80 units. The same can be true if one increases the operational cycle-time, as well. The cycle-time is just the inverse of the output rate (Equation 5.3). So, if the operation is creating 5 units per hour, the cycle-time would be 12 minutes per unit. Increasing the operational cycle time reduces the output rate, which reduces the realized output.

$$\textbf{cycle-time} = \frac{\textbf{1}}{\textbf{operation rate}} \qquad 5.3$$

Thus, organizations can prevent themselves from realizing the expected output by either reducing the number of hours worked through lower utilization or reducing the operation rate. Comparing

EXHIBIT 5.4

Availability of capacity directly influences what can be expected of a process.

Expected Availability (hours)	Expected Capacity (units)
24	120
20	100
16	80
10	50
8	40

realized capacity to expected capacity will create efficiency measures. Developing ratios comparing expected output to realized output, such as the one found in Equation 5.4, can begin to help managers understand their capacity and how it is being used. The efficiency measure helps the manager understand the fact that the operation is capable of producing more than the operators are getting from it. Two problems can arise from this situation, and the reader must pay very close attention to these issues. The two problems are:

- If efficiency is not at desired levels because of operational issues and there is ultimately demand for the product, the organization may improve its operational and financial performance by increasing the efficiency of the operation. May is the operative word, because unless the particular operation being considered constrains output in some way, lack of efficiency will not necessarily impact the overall process output.

- If efficiency is less than desired because there is not enough demand for the product and the operation is not operating as a result, there might be too much capacity. The mathematical complement of efficiency is loss (Equation 5.5). The operator is either doing value-adding work or it is not. Loss represents capacity that is available but is not being used. When the operation is not active, time is lost and there might have been investments made to ensure the capacity amount that is currently not being used. These investments, too, are lost. This is evident when reviewing the table in Exhibit 5.5. As the realized capacity and, therefore, efficiency go down, the losses increase. If there is not demand for the product, the loss may represent an overinvestment in capacity. In other words, high loss amounts where there is limited product demand represents a situation where the organization has too much capacity for its demand.

| EXHIBIT 5.5 | | |

Operational losses can often require additional capacity to be purchased or may lead to losses in output levels.

Expected Capacity	Realized Capacity	Loss
80	80	0
80	70	12.5%
80	60	25.0%
80	50	37.5%
80	40	50.0%
80	30	62.5%
80	20	75.0%
80	10	87.5%
80	0	100.0%

$$\text{operation efficiency} = \frac{\text{realized capacity}}{\text{expected capacity}} \qquad 5.4$$

$$\text{loss} = 1 - \text{operational efficiency}$$
$$= 1 - \frac{\text{realized capacity}}{\text{expected capacity}} \qquad 5.5$$

Managing the efficiency of an operation is very important because the efficiency impacts the relative amount of capacity that the organization must have. For organizations that have inefficient operations, they must overinvest in capacity to get the desired output in situations where there is excessive demand or even to meet current demand. An organization whose operations are 80% efficient, for instance, may only get 32 hours of a 40-hour work week out of its resources. It may pay for 40 hours. To get the 40 hours of work from its operations, it may actually have to ensure 50 hours of capacity to get 40 good hours. The impact of inefficient operations is clearly represented in Exhibit 5.6, where one can see that the amount of capacity required to get 40 hours

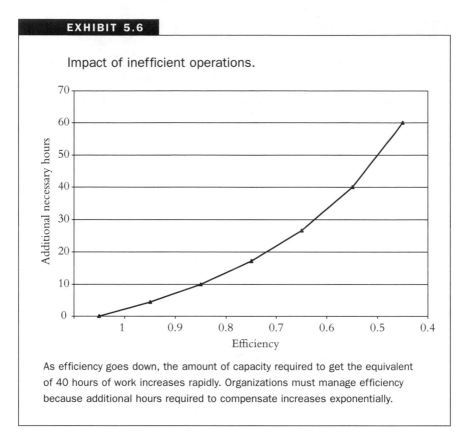

EXHIBIT 5.6

Impact of inefficient operations.

As efficiency goes down, the amount of capacity required to get the equivalent of 40 hours of work increases rapidly. Organizations must manage efficiency because additional hours required to compensate increases exponentially.

of work from an operation increases exponentially as loss increases linearly.

Another key issue to consider when managing efficiency is the definition of output. Output should be assumed to represent good, useable output product. Creating poor-quality output should not be included in the output of the operation and, therefore, should be considered as lost capacity. This definition should be used for both the expected and the realized capacity. Designing losses into processes, especially when determining the expected capacity, hides the loss itself and opportunities for operational improvement. It will also ultimately inflate the capacity requirements leading to a potential overspending on capacity.

To manage capacity effectively, one should seek an efficiency ratio of as close to one, or 100%, as possible. Managers have multiple degrees of freedom that will allow them to improve the efficiency rating. These degrees of freedom represent options that managers have that will enable them to change their operations while keeping their eyes on 100% efficiency. When considering the efficiency ratio itself, it can only be improved by increasing the numerator, which is the realized capacity. Reducing the denominator would be mathematically acceptable, too. However, the denominator cannot be reduced without impacting the numerator.

Increasing the numerator is an effective tool when not having the overall capacity constrains output. This is only an issue for processes that create output for which there is a tangible *who*, meaning a buying customer. Having a *who* suggests that there is demand for the product. No *who* creates capacity requirements that may have a negative impact on the organization from an operational perspective and a financial perspective (costs and working capital may increase whereas revenues do not). This should be avoided whenever possible.

The reasons for increasing efficiency and when one chooses to do so are extremely important. Although it may seem obvious to some, existing measures and philosophies often lead organizations to solutions that are counter to effective capacity management. Managers regularly seek realized capacity improvements to operations that are not constraining output or for which there is little or no demand. This is evident in organizations that manage by departments and do not take a process-oriented point of view. If every process were in its own department and if each department manager is required to improve the realized capacity of their capacity, he or she is going to do what he or she can to improve this value. What if, however, there is no demand? How often do performance measures take lack of demand into account? This decision to arbitrarily improve realized capacity can lead to overproduction, which can tie up working capital and increase the lead time of the overall process. What should really happen in this case is that expected capacity should be reduced to align more closely with the demand expectations placed on the process and, therefore, on the operation.

Increasing Realized Capacity by Increasing Efficiency

The difference between realized capacity and expected capacity is the fact that expected capacity assumes 100% utilization and assumes no variances to the cycle-time. It is the perfect world. Realized capacity, therefore, is defined by considering the utilization of the equipment and the actual measured cycle-time that might be reduced or, in some cases, increased during operations (Equation 5.6). The increase in cycle-time might result from inefficient tasks associated with the operation, inefficient layout, workers with less-than-desired skill levels, and many other causal factors. The same can create the opposite effect where an efficient layout or a more highly skilled worker can operate at levels higher than the standard cycle-time expectations.

$$\textbf{realized capacity} = \textbf{utilization} \times \textbf{realized cycle-time} \times \textbf{availability}$$
$$\textbf{realized cycle-time} = \textbf{\% standard cycle-time}$$

5.6

Efficiency as a measure, therefore, is influenced by the utilization of the equipment and variances to cycle-time. As shown in Equation 5.7, the standard cycle-time and the availability are going to be the same in the numerator and the denominator. Since they are the same, neither influences the efficiency of the operation. The efficiency, therefore, is only impacted by that which is different in the numerator and the denominator. The differences are created by the utilization and the cycle-time variance. By measuring each, the manager can determine what the efficiency of the operation is.

$$\text{Efficiency} = \frac{\text{realized capacity}}{\text{expected capacity}} \qquad\qquad 5.7$$

$$= \frac{\text{utilization} \times \text{realized cycle-time} \times \text{availability}}{\text{standard cycle-time} \times \text{availability}}$$

$$= \frac{\text{utilization} \times \% \text{ achieved} \times \text{standard cycle-time} \times \text{availability}}{\text{standard cycle-time} \times \text{availability}}$$

$$= \text{utilization} \times \% \text{ achieved}$$

There are, therefore, two fundamental ways to improve efficiency by increasing realized capacity:

- Increase utilization
- Reduce cycle-time variances if negative or increase them if positive

Increasing utilization involves eliminating the factors that reduce utilization. The interactions of entities, such as less-than-desirable employee task design or execution may cause the equipment to be down as it waits for the labor. Likewise, lack of materials can lead to lower than desirable utilization of the equipment as can excessive changeover or set-up time and creating output with unacceptable quality. In this case, the organization should spend time understanding the causal factors for operation underutilization and work diligently to fix them.

A cycle-time variance occurs when the actual measured cycle-time varies from that which is expected. For example, if the expected or standard cycle-time is 12 minutes per part, but the realized cycle-time is 14 minutes per part, the capacity is reduced by almost 0.75 units per hour, or 6 units per 8-hour shift. There are many factors that could impact why this measure is off. Managers and engineers must spend time determining why the variance exists, including the possibility that the standard measure is incorrect or unrealistic.

Increasing Realized Capacity without Increasing Efficiency

There may be times when an organization needs more capacity regardless of the efficiency level. In times of fast growth, high demand, or certain levels and types of competitive situations, organizations often choose to quickly increase their realized capacity and focus on efficiency later. There are two ways that you can increase realized capacity without increasing efficiency. You do so by increasing the factors that are common to both the numerator and the denominator:

- Standard cycle-time
- Availability

Standard cycle-time is a component that one can address to increase realized capacity without increasing efficiency. Only the variance between realized and expected cycle-time can impact efficiency. Actions to increase the standard cycle-time will increase both the realized and the expected cycle-time. Reducing the standard cycle-time is the same as increasing the output per unit of time. In essence, reducing cycle-time involves making the output at a faster rate. This can be done in multiple ways. Products can be designed for reduced cycle-time. Non–value-adding tasks can be eliminated. Faster machines can be purchased. Personal experience has found that the late Shigeo Shingo, one of the fathers of just-in-time manufacturing, had excellent approaches and ideas that can be applied to reduce cycle-time.[2]

Finally, available time can be increased. Available time increases can occur by eliminating that which limits available time in the first place. So, if available time is limited by labor, scheduling additional shifts, or increasing the length of current shifts can increase the amount of available time that exists.

Reducing Expected Capacity

Reducing expected capacity involves reducing either the operation rate or the availability of an operation. With either, you are changing a variable that exists in both the numerator and the denominator of the efficiency equation. The result of changing the expected capacity, therefore, does not impact efficiency, but it may have an impact on the organization from a financial point of view. Whether the operation rate has an impact on financial performance is determined by what enables it. For example, if homogeneous capacity (see Chapter 2) makes up the capacity, eliminating some of the capacity may create financial improvements for the organization in the form of cost-cutting. Similarly, if availability requires capacity components that maintains high costs or increase its costs, reducing those components can lead to cost reductions for the organization.

Organizations must be fairly strict about how they determine the cost components tied to capacity. For example, if availability reduction eliminates half of a shift, it may not result in cost reduction because the organization may be required to pay for a whole shift. The same holds true for saving part of a machine. You cannot claim machine-based cost savings by reducing capacity by half of a machine.

The approach for nonconstraining resources that includes those where overall demand is either sufficient or not sufficient, would be to reduce the expected capacity. With lower expected output, the organization can begin to focus on those components that improve efficiency without creating adverse effects, such as excess inventory or requiring unnecessary capacity of other sorts. Using smaller capacity values at 100% utilization helps the organization manage capacity more effectively because it knows exactly what it needs in capacity to meet what is expected. In general, it is better to seek 100% utilization and manage availability.

Operations do not exist in a vacuum. In the context of a process, one must manage the whole process and the expected output of the process rather than the individual operations. The previous sections focused on helping you understand the basics of operations dynamics. This basic understanding of operations will be regularly called upon as we consider how operations interact to create the process output.

Consider the process in Exhibit 5.7 where there is raw material going into the primary conversion operation. This conversion operation has an expected capacity output of 6 units per hour. The output units from this operation feed the secondary operation, which processes at the rate of 5 units per hour. Finally, there is final assembly, which is capable of processing at 8 units per hour. Final assembly will be assumed to assemble parts purchased on the outside with the items created by the previous two operations in the process.

The expected capacity of this process is 5 units per hour. Although the other operations are faster and, therefore, have more output rate capacity, the slowest operation limits the total output capacity of the process. The expected capacity of the process, therefore, is limited to

EXHIBIT 5.7

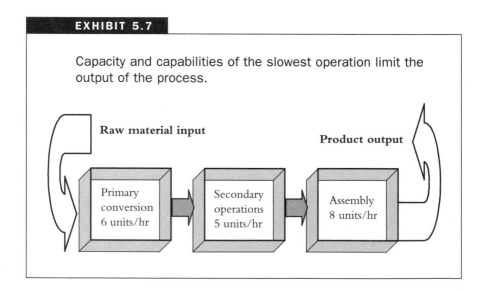

Capacity and capabilities of the slowest operation limit the output of the process.

the expected output rate capacity of the slowest operation. That would be the secondary operation in this case.

To determine the expected output rate capacity, one would apply Equation 5.8 (which repeats Equation 5.2) to the operation with the lowest total output rate. You must calculate the lowest *total* output rate because the second operation might have output rate of 5 units per hour for each labor-machine capacity, but there may be two sets for a total of 10 units per hour output rate. Determining the realized capacity works the same as it does for the operation. For the process, one looks at how much output was created over a period of time and compares this value to what was expected. This will give a process efficiency measure and its complement—the loss, that will help managers understand whether they are getting out of their processes what they are expecting.

$$\frac{\text{expected output capacity}}{\text{day}} = \frac{\text{expected availability (hours)}}{\text{day}} \times \frac{\text{unit}}{\text{hour}} \qquad 5.8$$

The difference that you find managing processes and not with managing operations centers on trying to close the negative variances that exist. With the operation, you looked at the utilization and the cycle-time variance to find out where the problems might exist. You would consider doing the same with processes, but the technique for doing so is a bit different. You first look to the slowest operation. You then look at downstream operations, to find out if there were any problems at operations that are after the slowest operation in the process, to find out if another operation is negatively impacting output.

Analyzing the Slowest Operation

The total capacity is limited by the slowest operation. If the realized capacity is lower than the expected capacity, the maximum possible value for the process goes down by the same amount. Hence, if, for some reason, the operation realizes only 3 units per hour rather than the expected 5 units per hour, the total throughput capability of the process is reduced to 3. So, the first place to look when trying to improve the realized capacity is the slowest operations.

When analyzing the slowest operation, one would focus on the utilization and cycle-time variances to determine probable cause. The cause might be issues described earlier in the operations sections. The cause could also be upstream processes that feed the slowest operation. Low efficiencies and poor planning at upstream operations may create situations where the slowest operation is starved for materials. So, although its cycle-time variance might be zero or even positive, low utilization might bring the overall process capacity down.

The objective, as will be seen in Chapter 7, will be to ensure that the slowest operation is as close to 100% efficient for demand that exceeds process output capability. In the latter part of the book, where issues such as planning and scheduling capacity are highlighted, techniques are discussed for ensuring that the proper flow of materials exists to get the most out of the operational capacity, especially the slow operations.

Downstream Processes

When analyzing downstream operations, you should look to find out how and why the rate of output from the slowest operation is not sustained. By definition, the downstream operations will have more output capacity than the slowest operation. Therefore, it should not be an issue for the downstream operations to be able to sustain the pace of the slowest operation. However, with the focus often being on the slowest operations, managers may find that the downstream operations are lacking the appropriate attention to detail that will be necessary to ensure high levels of output. Therefore, the objective of looking at the downstream processes is to refocus efforts on trying to find the reason for the drop-off in capacity and to repair it, so that it does not have negative financial and operational impacts on the organization.

Other Process Types

There are other process types that have some of the same characteristics as conversion processes. Those considered here are operational processes and concept development processes. Operational processes often have a similar look and feel to conversion processes, as they are often very linear, and it is often desired that the processes operate efficiently and effectively. Concept-related processes might be linear, but they can also be nonlinear. They can also be very cerebral, which can have a major impact on how quickly a product can be created. This section will discuss both types of processes, and that will lead to the close of the chapter.

Operational Processes

Operational processes constitute most of the activities within an organization. From hiring through purchasing, accounting, and other activities, to get something done in the organization, there is often a process to do it, however well defined the process may be. From a capacity-entity perspective, organizational processes tend to require space, as there are workers who make up the processes, and they have space requirements of their own (Exhibit 5.8). Such processes tend to require office space since they are often relatively labor intensive. How the process depends on equipment, specifically, is determined by the process. For example, an accounts payable process that physically creates checks may depend on the equipment required to do so. Processes that create physical products will have a material component to their operation. Whether IT plays a role depends, too, on the nature of the process and the operations. Many organizations are finding that many technologies are taking the human component out of decision-making, which can shift or even reduce the labor capacity requirements for

EXHIBIT 5.8

Operational processes tend to emphasize space and labor due to the often-required human component.

Entities at Work	Likelihood
Space	Medium-High
Labor	Low-High
Equipment	Low-Medium
IT	Low-High
Materials	Low

many organizations. Additionally, technology can often work more quickly and offload some of the work performed by the process, which can sometimes lead to lower lead time.

Operational processes have many of the same issues as conversion processes. In fact, in many ways, they are conversion processes. To buy something, someone may begin with the operation associated with finding the product. There might be multiple searches associated with finding the right product at the right price and location. They may search catalogues, look on the Internet, or ask someone about contracts that may be in place to buy the items. One may then create a purchase requisition for the items. The requisition goes to purchasing where the order is created and purchasing calls in the order. The order is received, checked, and delivered to the person who ordered the product.

In an example such as this, the same rules apply for this process as it does for the manufacturing process. The output rate is determined by the slowest operation. If the actual ordering of items is the slowest operation, it will dictate the rate at which the purchasing can place orders. This may have an impact on the lead time because the constraint may lead to a queue that, as discussed earlier, has a negative time impact. Since requests may come in from multiple locations within the organization, and because the demand and the process are independent, management does not have much control over managing the entire process. The purchasing department would have to decide how much capacity is needed given the organization's financial situation and the importance for quick turnaround. Clearly, the organization must pay for its capacity and, therefore, must perform the proper analyses to ensure the proper return for its investments. The organization also has the option to try to either speed the process or to take away some of the demand being placed on the purchasing department. Software-based procurement tools perform this function. For certain items, the person buying the product can go onto an intranet, find the items, and order them without going through the purchasing department. This offloads the demand placed on the purchasing department, leading to the potential to reduce the total capacity in the department, and also speeds the process.

The same holds true for processes such as accounts payable and accounts receivable. These two processes have a major impact on working capital, as will be seen in Chapter 6. Organizations will want to ensure that both processes are aligned with the strategy of the organization. In these cases, one may even manage the process as one would manage a conversion process. The focus would be on throughput and effective management of the capacity. Issues such as availability become important when missing one day of receivables can mean approximately three million in cash flow for a $1 billion company.

Processes such as receivables and payables can be managed similarly to how one manages conversion processes. The operation output rates can be determined and used to decide how to achieve the required output levels. Instead of looking to external demand to determine throughput rates, the organization's strategy is the determinant. So, if the objective is to reduce receivables, time and quantity targets for processes, such as billing, can be established and used as standards or benchmarks. The time targets can be used as a basis for lead time–oriented issues, such as queue time. The quantity targets can be used as a basis for throughput-related decisions. The throughput decisions will be tied to the operational constraint and to effectively managing the operational constraints to ensure maximum availability and utilization.

Development Processes

Development processes are the same as conversion processes and operational processes in many ways, and they are different in other ways. They are similar because development processes often have a linear component to them. When developing a new product design, for instance, there are certain steps that must occur sequentially. One cannot start building physical products without the design, engineering, and process information necessary to do so. The processes are different for two major reasons. First, the processes are more cerebral and less tied to that which could make the process highly predictable. The second difference is that although there is a basic sequence of events, the process is less tied to the chronology of events and the events themselves as the other types of processes. In terms of how they consume capacity, development processes are highly variable. From a space perspective, that which is required will depend on the process and the organization. For example, processes that have teams that are co-located have greater space requirements than those who have teams that telecommute. They can clearly be labor intensive because it is the brainpower of the labor capacity that influences the activities and the output of the process. The equipment and IT requirements are tied to the type of process. For example, when developing an organization strategy or when developing measurement scorecards, there may be no equipment requirements at all. IT may be required for research and dissemination purposes. When designing an automobile, equipment may be necessary to build prototype models and to help model the production process. Additionally, IT is heavily used for design, computer-based testing, such as finite element analysis–based testing, and creating computer-based manufacturing programs. The result is a wide-ranging use of capacity depending on purpose (Exhibit 5.9).

When developing and managing development processes, it is much harder to focus on operation rates and lead times because the nature and scope of the work is so different. Two cars will have different development cycles, regardless of how similar they may appear to be, due to variations in the operations or activities that make up the process. There are multiple teams of various sizes for each activity.[3] Each may have different management approaches and the team members have different competencies. To predict exactly how long it will take to do a particular test is impossible. The objective, therefore, is to try to determine what options exist for both reducing operation-activity time and improving lead time performance.

What many organizations do in situations such as this is to "time box" the activities. Time-boxing is a method of controlling the maximum amount of time that an activity can take. You may say, for instance, "Since this particular activity can take anywhere from 30 minutes to 3 hours to complete, we will give you 2 hours to complete your tasks." By setting time constraints on activities, organizations can manage the total time that an activity and, therefore, the entire process can take.

EXHIBIT 5.9

Capacity depending on purpose.

Entities at work	Likelihood
Space	Low-Medium
Labor	High
Equipment	Low-Medium
IT	Low-High
Materials	Low

Development processes are highly labor intensive. Requirements placed on other entities depend on the required output.

Another technique often used to reduce the total lead time for development processes is to overlap activities. Since the process is often fairly flexible, starting on activities as early in the process may have an impact on overall lead time. With product development, for instance, organizations often break up the product being created and give each component the ability to move through the organization at its own pace. When managing a process such as this, one tries to determine what information the next step needs, so that work can start immediately at subsequent operations. Work begins, therefore, on subsequent activities before the first activity is complete. Although there are some risks with this approach, oftentimes organizations find that the rewards far outweigh the risks. If organizations can get products or strategies to the market faster, it might be of financial benefit to do so. If there were a major problem with the output from the former activity and the problem is identified at a downstream operation, it is identified more quickly and can be corrected without significant and, therefore, wasteful work being done. The idea of having concurrent activities going on within a process creates benefits, such as lowered development lead time, and can often reduce the impact of changes to the product by a significant amount.

Constraints will still exist. It will still take longer to develop certain products than others and the overall product is limited by the item with the longest lead time. The constraints must still be managed the same way. Increasing the capacity of the constraint to create greater capacity is one option. As with other processes, outsourcing may be another option. All solutions, however, must be designed and implemented to ensure the maximum quality product in the allotted time.

This chapter has focused on creating processes. Financial issues had not been introduced to this point. To gain a better understanding of processes and to prepare to manage and optimize them, we must introduce the concept of financial dynamics. This will set the stage for the last two chapters of the book, which are focused on process optimization and the process for managing capacity.

Endnotes

[1] The term product is used generically as the output of a process.

[2] See for example, Shigeo Shingo, *The Sayings of Shigeo Shingo: Key Strategies for Plant Improvement,* trans. Andrew Dillon (Boston: Productivity Press, 1985, 1987).

[3] Activity will be used for development processes rather than operation. Although they are conceptually the same thing, activity seems more appropriate for this use.

CHAPTER 6

Financial Dynamics of Capacity Management

After reading this chapter, you will be able to:

- Define the concept of financial dynamics
- Describe the components of financial dynamics
- Describe the importance of cash flow measures

Introduction

This chapter will provide an understanding of how capacity impacts the financial dynamics of an organization. This is arguably the most important chapter, because it highlights how capacity decisions that you will make impact your organization's financial results. Oftentimes, capacity is managed with either a purely operational focus or with measures that do not reflect the true financial dynamics of the organization as they relate to capacity. This results in actions that do not provide the anticipated returns, and in many cases, provide negative results for organizations. This chapter will begin to introduce the reader to the financial dynamics of the organization. Included in the financial dynamics are the revenue dynamics, cost dynamics, and working capital dynamics. The focus is on bottom line results because these results are the only ones that matter when trying to manage revenues and costs. Although intradivisional revenue and cost transfers are nice, they do not impact the bottom line.

In the first chapter, the emphasis was on identifying the magnitude of the impact that capacity has on financial measures. In this chapter, we will understand *why* capacity has an impact on the organization's financial dynamics, how the impact occurs, and *to what extent* capacity can impact the financial dynamics at a high level. The chapter will begin with a fundamental discussion of financial dynamics so that there is a common understanding of what it is that we are trying to impact with our decision making and how it is impacted. The financial dynamics will be based on cash flow types of measures for two reasons. First, cash-based measures, such as profit and the cash flow, are extremely important measures that managers, shareholders, and analysts watch very closely. Second, cash flow itself is a measure that is often most closely aligned with a firm's market value.[1] Simply, when analysts determine the market value of a company, one of the key values to consider is the net present value of the future cash flows for the organization. Although the details are beyond the scope of this book, the fundamental concept is important to consider when managing capacity. One can be assured to the greatest extent possible which capacity management actions can positively or negatively impact the cash flow and, therefore, the market value of the organization.

What Are Financial Dynamics?

Financial dynamics represent the change in certain finance-based numbers as a result of an organization's operating conditions or decisions. In this book, the realms of financial dynamics are capacity and capacity management. The objective is to help the reader understand how their management of capacity and the decisions that they make will impact key financial measures. As discussed above, focus will only be on cash flow–based financial dynamics. As such, the key measures that we will discuss are:

- Income
- Expenses
- Working capital

Income

For the purpose of this book, income will represent the money received from both operating and nonoperating sources. Operating income represent the money received as a result of performing the functions for which the organization is in business. Hence, consulting revenues are operating income for consulting firms, just as selling automobiles provides operating income for automotive companies. Nonoperating income is received for reasons outside of how the organization would typically generate income. An example would be a consulting firm that has invested its cash and now receives money from its investments.

Since this book focuses on the cash flow management, only revenues considered at the income statement level are appropriate to measure. This means that we are only looking at income coming in from outside of the organization. Budget transfers within the organization are not considered increases in income. Therefore, serving another department or division more effectively without bringing in money from outside of the organization is not considered to be an increase in income. The reason is simply that the cash flow of the organization is not impacted by the action. Only the cash flow of the department or the division is affected. Therefore, such activities are outside of the scope of the discussion in this book.

Expenses

Expenses here represent the money that must be paid to others outside of the company. When the money leaves the organization in whatever form, it will be considered an expense. Budget transfers, as with income, do not count as expenses to the organization. They should only be considered expenses if they can be traced directly to the income statement level. If the value does not show up at that level, it should not be considered as an expense.

Expenses are often difficult to manage, control, and discuss. Many of the approaches used to manage expenses and costs use allocation techniques that confuse the person doing the analysis, often unknowingly. Statements such as, "increasing the productivity reduces costs," and "the more we make, the cheaper it is," reflect the misunderstanding of how organizations incur expenses. Increasing productivity does not reduce expenses. It creates options. Output can be increased or input can be decreased, both of which *may* increase profitability. Another choice is to do nothing with the improvement, which leads to a negative net investment, as expenses were incurred with no improvement in income or expenses. Additionally, it cannot be cheaper to make more when looking at the expenses at the income statement level. At least the same labor is involved; more materials and time are being utilized. It just does not make sense. Bottom-line costs cannot go down as more is done.[2]

Not convinced? Ask yourself the following question: how can it be cheaper to make the third widget than the second, the twelfth less than the eleventh? As more is done, more materials and utilities are used to make the additional products than fewer. Resources are not being paid any less. From a bottom-line perspective, it costs the organization more to make the third widget than it does to make the second. It cannot be cheaper for the organization to make more. It is not a mathematical possibility. Think, therefore, about all of the decisions that are made with respect to capacity that does not reflect this knowledge. How many times is more inventory purchased because it is *cheaper*? This view is created by allocating costs and creating a "cost per something" ratio that does not occur on the bottom line.

Cost allocation creates a view of cost dynamics that, although mathematically valid, is impractical when managing the bottom line. Consider the setup of a machine. Assume that it costs the organization $1,000 to set up a machine. Allocation techniques attempt to spread this cost by giving a piece of the set-up cost to each unit produced as a result of the set-up. So, if one unit is produced, it gets the entire $1,000. If 10 units are produced, each unit gets $100. If 100, each unit gets $10. The amount for each unit is determined by dividing the total cost by the number of units. Looking at this mathematically, one would assume that the more that is made, the cheaper is the cost per unit and, therefore, the total cost (see Exhibit 6.1).

This is not reflected by the bottom line, however. The bottom line sees that the $1,000 exists regardless of the number of units produced. The bottom line reflects an action that costs the organization $1,000. The interesting thing is that more materials and other variable inputs are consumed when making more products. If one cost is constant and the

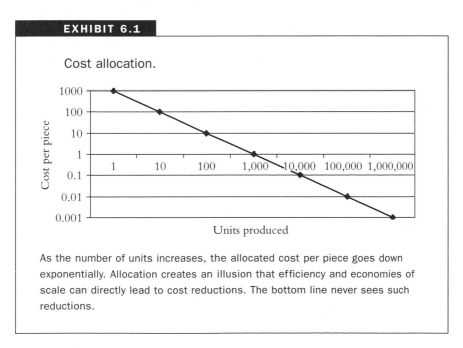

EXHIBIT 6.1

Cost allocation.

As the number of units increases, the allocated cost per piece goes down exponentially. Allocation creates an illusion that efficiency and economies of scale can directly lead to cost reductions. The bottom line never sees such reductions.

other costs are either constant or increasing, it must be concluded that costs remain the same at a minimum and likely *increase* as production increases. Widely used cost-accounting techniques, including activity-based costing, would suggest that costs go down. The reality suggests that costs go up. Which makes intuitive sense? Which assumption does your organization use when analyzing costs?

The purist might argue that if one allocates the costs to the unit and multiplies by the number of units, the bottom-line cost remains the same. This is a fact. However, the problem arises when one uses the allocated cost information to make decisions. This is how we come to the conclusion that it is cheaper to make more, but the assumption is incorrect. Often, business cases are based on this fact, and the savings amounts identified are incorrect. Consider a call center whose capacity a manager is trying to manage more effectively. Assume that the manager determines that the resource costs of the department are $1 million per year when handling approximately 100,000 calls per year.

In situations such as this, one can determine a cost-per-call value of $10 per call ($1 million ÷ 100,000 calls). The organization decides to invest in a web-based call center solution where customers can answer the questions that they may have at the web site. It is assumed that half of the calls will be eliminated as a result of the solution. Therefore, the call center might only answer 50,000 calls per year. You can see where this is going. Ninety-nine percent of the business cases that I have seen to this point would show that there would be a savings of $500,000 (saving 50,000 calls at $10 per call). This does not happen by itself. If the organization does not act to reduce the call center staff capacity by 50% or more, it will never see the $500,000. This is often the case.[3] If management does not reduce the infrastructure, the cost per call has now gone up. What does this tell us? Not much. The important information comes more in understanding the cost of the capacity necessary to provide a certain output level than it does from determining the cost per unit. It is a subtle difference as stated but a huge difference when acted on. The former suggests relationship and the latter suggests allocation. With the former, one understands that there is $1 million required to make 100,000 calls. If the call volume is changed, what must occur to maintain similar use of the capacity? The dollar value of the capacity must change accordingly if at all. It can be realized that if the organization can handle more calls for $1 million, it would be better off. Or, if the organization can increase the $1 million figure at a slower rate than the rate of increase of the calls, it is better off. If the number of calls is reduced, the capacity must be reduced at a similar or faster rate. What is required of the organization and the resulting next steps become obvious. However, in case after case, the technique of allocating costs results in a belief that since it costs $10 per call, if the total number of calls is reduced, the cost goes down. *This just does not happen.*

When we believe that it is cheaper to make more, we make decisions such as producing too much or buying too much in the name of saving money when, in fact, we are increasing costs, not decreasing them. Many companies with excess inventory capacity have realized this fact. Additionally, capital is tied up in materials that are adding no value to their operations. If the allocation of cost via division (e.g., $/unit) creates negative behavior, why do it?

To help with the understanding of expense dynamics, we will use three categories to represent expense types:

- Resources
- Actions
- Items

Each expense type has dynamics that can be tied directly to the bottom line, which is necessary to model and manage the bottom line effectively.

Each is a nonallocated expense, which makes modeling and managing the bottom line much easier and more accurate than when using traditional tools. Why? Simply, as suggested above, the traditional allocation techniques do not reflect what is going on from the bottom-line perspective, so one cannot use them to model the bottom line. Each will now be discussed in turn.

Resources

Resource costs are costs that exist regardless of what goes on in the organization. If all activities stopped, resources would comprise the remaining expenses. Therefore, labor, purchased space, and bought or leased equipment, and many materials are resource costs. In fact, practically all capacity costs are resource costs.

Actions

Action costs are costs that are seen as incrementally increasing in expenses as the action is performed. An example would be a long-distance call or a shipment where money must leave the organization every time the action is performed. It is important to distinguish an action cost here from an activity cost that may be used in activity-based costing, or ABC. From a capacity management perspective, activity costs in ABC reflect the *costs* of tasks, operations, or processes. So, because these tasks and operations are comprised mostly of resources that are basically fixed costs, the activities to which the resources are assigned do not change in cost when measured at the bottom line. One simply adjusts the allocation of a resource to tasks, operations, or processes, which creates the perception of changing costs after the allocation takes place. However, the bottom line does not see it. The so-called changing costs are, in fact, a part of a zero-sum game.

Actions that do not cause money to leave the organization are not considered expenses. This is a key point to understand with capacity management, because costs are often allocated to assign costs to a person's job or to a task. So, using this approach, if someone makes $12/hour, it may be assumed that each hour that the person spends doing something that is a part of his or her job costs the organization $12. In fact, it does not. Often, if a clerk spends 10 hours per week searching for information, it is assumed to cost the company $120. However, this $120 is already tied to the person's salary, so, as long as the amount is paid, it really does not matter what the person does with his time from a bottom-line perspective. Reducing the search time by 50% will not reduce the costs by $60, because the clerk still gets $12/hour whether he or she is searching for information.[4]

Item

Items are materials purchased to be converted and sold. These are items that are purchased for a specific purpose. A specific garage door that is purchased for a house being built is an item. Material capacity is not considered an item cost because it is purchased in anticipation of some sort of nonspecific demand. Materials that are purchased as reserves suggest that they are providing some sort of capacity or capability to meet future demand. Hence, just because there is an item that is either considered raw material or is a component of some type does not mean

TIPS & TECHNIQUES

Understanding the dynamics of costs and how they are impacted by capacity is of the utmost importance when managing capacity. Look around your organization and determine to what extent the cost dynamics of capacity are understood. Before implementing an effective capacity management program, make sure that the organization understands financial parameters that it will manage.

that it is considered an item cost automatically. It depends on why the item was purchased in the first place. In other words, *what* it is is not important. Its purpose is important.

Working Capital

Working capital represents the current assets and current liabilities for which an organization is responsible. Simply, working capital represents the difference between current assets and current liabilities (see Equation 6.1). The current assets that we will focus on here are accounts receivable, or "receivables" for short, and inventory. Cash is another major current asset type but is assumed to be a given. The current liability focused on here is accounts payable, or just "payables." Each is briefly discussed.

$$\text{working capital} = \text{current assets} - \text{current liabilities} \qquad 6.1$$

Receivables

Receivables are simply the cash that is expected to be collected from customers. When properly calculated, it differs from sales because in reality, not everyone pays, and there are sometimes discounts given for those who pay more quickly. However, for quick analysis purposes, the sales number is used to assess the approximate size of receivables.

If someone owes you money, it is nice to say that he or she owes you, but, in reality, you want the money. With the collection comes an increase in your cash flow. This cash can be reinvested or used to pay debt. The same is basically true for organizations. The objective should be to collect money as quickly as possible to increase the amount of cash available to the organization. With this money in their hands comes opportunities to reinvest the cash, which can potentially increase overall cash flow even further.

A measure that one can use to determine how effectively receivables are being managed is to determine the days of sales that are outstanding. This number can be compared to averages in the industry or to its standard payment terms to determine how effectively its cash collections process is. The ratio used to determine this value is the total receivables divided by the average sales per day (see Equation 6.2). The values for receivables and sales are both available off of an organization's financial statements. Sales can be divided by 365 to determine the average sales per day. Once the ratio is established, one can begin to assess how effective the processes associated with billing and receiving are functioning.

$$\text{days of sales outstanding} = \frac{\text{receivables}}{\text{sales/day}} \qquad 6.2$$

Two quick assessment opportunities involve comparing days sales outstanding with competitors' values and with your own terms. Assume that an organization has $9 million in receivables from sales of $100,000 per day. This organization would have 90 days of receivables. Now, assume that the industry average is 75 days. If this organization were to get to 75 days of sales outstanding, it would free $1.5 million in cash (see Equation 6.3).

$$\begin{aligned}
\text{receivables} &= \frac{\text{sales}}{\text{day}} \times \text{days of sales outstanding} \\
&= \$100,000 \times 75 \text{ days} \\
&= \$7.5 \text{ million} \qquad 6.3 \\
\text{freed cash} &= \text{original receivables} - \text{new receivables} \\
&= \$9 \text{ million} - \$7.5 \text{ million} \\
&= \$1.5 \text{ million}
\end{aligned}$$

Another objective that organizations can strive to achieve is to reduce its payment terms in general. This organization may have payment terms that expect full payment in 60 days. For every day that they reduce as they strive for their ultimate objective of 60 days, through the effective utilization of labor and IT capacity, they free up $100 thousand in cash.

Inventory

In addition to representing capacity to create products, inventory represents tied-up cash. An organization buys materials and hopes to turn the materials into products that they can sell to the market. Until the sales occur, the money invested is not really doing anything for the organization. The inventory exists in the forms of raw materials, work in progress, and finished goods, and as long as there is inventory, there is money that is tied up and not providing a return to the firm. The idea, therefore, is to figure out the most effective way to meet the demands of the market while tying up the cash for the shortest period of time. An effective way to do this is to manage the inventory levels to anticipated demand.

Inventory Levels

Inventory built to meet forecasted demand must be kept at levels that ensure the proper balance between desired financial results, including market valuation and service levels. The service level represents the percentage of orders that can be filled in the shortest, agreed-upon period of time. Oftentimes, organizations assume that there must be a 100% service level at all costs. The period of time that is used is often zero, suggesting that the product be kept in stock. The more inventory that is kept, the more it will cost the organization. More materials are required, and there might be incremental space and labor costs associated with storing and managing the materials, placing the inventory, and retrieving the inventory, as well. Regularly, however, organizations tend to build excess inventory, in case there is demand for the product. In many circumstances, this may not be the way to manage inventory because when one compares the costs and the benefits, the costs may not outweigh the benefits.

Determining Inventory Levels

Determining the right levels of inventory may not be an easy task. There is a lot of detailed information that one may want to understand before making this decision. Consider the demand patterns laid out in Exhibit 6.2. In this exhibit, demand over 48 periods is being considered. Note that this analysis is for illustrative purposes only and does not reflect the rigorous statistical analysis that should typically be performed to determine, with high confidence, the demand data and the respective conclusions that can be drawn from the data.

Exhibit 6.2 describes hypothetical demand levels for a fictitious company. This represents that which the market actually purchased from the company. The frequency reflects the number of times that the market demanded that amount. So, over 48 analysis periods, the market demanded 8 units 1 time, 10 units 18 times, 12 units 7 times, and so on. From this information, the approximate probability that the market will purchase a particular number of products can be determined. The probability that the market will demand 10 units in an arbitrary period, ignoring

---

EXHIBIT 6.2

Demand Patterns.

Actual demand	8	9	10	11	12	13	14	15	16	17	18
Frequency	1	8	18	11	7	1	0	0	1	0	1
Probability	2	17	37	23	15	2	0	0	2	0	2
Cumulative probability	2	19	56	79	94	96	96	96	98	98	100

To properly manage inventory levels, organizations must understand their demand patterns. With the frequency of occurrence, the resulting probability and cumulative probabilities create a total picture of demand.

issues such as seasonality or other trends, would be 37%. So, if the organization chose to have 10 units in inventory, it has a bit more than a one-in-three chance of correctly guessing the demand. Another value to look at is the cumulative probability. If the organization decides to maintain 10 units in inventory, it not only covers the fact that the demand may be 10, but it also covers the fact that the demand may be less than 10. In other words, having 10 in inventory covers the probability that the demand will be less than or equal to 10. Therefore, if the organization has 10 units in stock, it will cover 56% of the situations that it sees. Demand for 9 units occurs 17% of the time, and demand for 8 occurs 2% of the time. The total of the three is 56%. In 56% of the cases, therefore, it can meet demand, suggesting that the service level will be approximately 56%. The service level reflects the likelihood that the demand will be less than or equal to the amount of units in inventory.

In Exhibit 6.3, the service levels for varying levels of inventory are considered. The exhibit simply states the service level that one would have at different inventory levels. Hence, if 10 pieces were kept in inventory, the organization can expect to meet the demand 56% of the time. Notice a couple of important points. There are a couple of areas where, given the specifics of this data, keeping higher levels of inventory does not help. Keeping 16 pieces gives no better service than 17. Thirteen gives the same service as 15. Organizations must understand what the benefits are of carrying higher levels of inventory. As seen here and as is often the case, carrying more inventory may not provide additional financial benefits, and it ties up cash. The second key point focuses on what happens at 100% customer service levels. Suppose that under no circumstance will the demand go above 18. So, having 18 pieces ensures that the demand can be met 100% of the time. Many organizations who do not perform the proper inventory analysis end up carrying 21, 22, or

EXHIBIT 6.3

Service levels reflect the ability to fill orders out of inventory. It is directly related to the probability that demand is less than or equal to the inventory level.

Inventory Level	Service Level
8	2
9	19
10	56
11	79
12	94
13	96
14	96
15	96
16	98
17	98
18	100
19 and up	100

25 pieces of inventory, just in case. They get no more benefit out of it, but they do it, so that they can meet anticipated demand. Never mind that they can carry almost half of the inventory and meet the demand 95% of the time. Too much money is tied up for too long as organizations try to manage the service level. Carrying anything above 18 pieces is overkill and leads to poorer financial results.

The question is, in the absence of extraneous factors, how does one determine the correct inventory levels? The issue is one of comparing what the organization gains from having certain levels of inventory. For example, what happens if an order arrives and the product is not in inventory? If the product is not in inventory, the customers will either wait or they will not. The inventory level decision, therefore, will be impacted by issues such as:

- How critical is the article to the customer? If the product is critical for the customer, they may seek a replacement or develop one of their own. In either case, your company loses the revenue. This may or may not be a bad thing. It is a good thing if the cost of maintaining the high amounts of inventory and the support staff necessary to serve the customer is so high that it does not make financial sense to meet the demand. It is a bad thing if it causes a good customer to seek its products from another organization and the cost of supporting this particular customer-set is reasonable.

- Are there replacement products on the market? If there are replacement products on the market, whether critical or not, the customer may decide to go to a competitor for the product. Again, this represents lost revenues and the concern might be whether a good customer decides to take his or her business elsewhere. If there are not replacement products, the customer may choose to do without the product, create his or her own, or wait for yours. Although having customers wait on a product may be an enviable position, the organization may not want to upset the customers by forcing them to wait for products unless it is of benefit to the customer. If, for example, every time someone wants your product, they have to wait nine months, depending on the product, this may create a negative brand image for your company. This may impact sales for other products. If, however, the wait means some of the benefits that your company incurs are passed on to the customer with low prices, for instance, the result may be better received by the market.

- How much does it cost to maintain a certain level of inventory? This is a pretty controversial area, actually. There are a large number of techniques out there that supposedly determine the cost of inventory. Traditional costs may include the carrying cost of the inventory (holding costs), the cost of incurring shortages (opportunity costs), and the cost of replenishing inventory (ordering costs).[5] Although this makes sense, how one calculates the cost is what is important. Again, we are focusing on the cash flow impact, so let us look at each one in turn.

Using Elsayed and Boucher's *Analysis and Control of Production Systems* as a somewhat typical, yet thorough, example, the authors break up inventory carrying costs into four areas.[6] The *opportunity cost*, according to the authors, represents income forgone because money is not in an interest-bearing account. This is nonoperating income and not a cost. *Storage and space costs* represent the cost of storing inventory. Costs are typically allocated to the space occupied by the inventory. Although storage must be considered, it does not have to be in a typical fashion. Space is capacity, and until one has to pay more to get extra space, there is no incremental increase in costs. For example, if an organization leases warehouse space and the warehouse is 40% utilized, space costs do not increase until the maximum capacity is reached. At that point, the organization must increase its capacity. The cost to do so is an organizational cost of doing business and not the cost of maintaining the inventory itself.[7] *Taxes and insurance premiums* are payments that must be made, and if they are tied to the amount of inventory, the cost is a fair one. *The cost of obsolescence* represents the cost of an item in inventory that has become obsolete. Obsolescence cost is an interesting idea. If materials are purchased and they become obsolete, is the cost counted twice? Inventory that becomes obsolete is a bad situation because the money is lost and because the organization may have to replace it with new material capacity. If they do replace the inventory, they pay more for creating and having the additional inventory capacity. It is somewhat like buying cereal. The cost of the cereal is the cost of the cereal, and there is no cost of throwing it away. If the cereal grows stale, the parents may have to buy extra cereal to make it through an equal number of breakfasts. This cost may or may not be incurred, as the parent can put his or her foot down and say that no more cereal will be purchased if the kids cannot finish what he or she buys. Effective inventory management and demand planning should be used to reduce obsolescence, but once purchased, the money is gone, and it is up to the organization to figure out how to make money from its investment and whether to make additional investments in inventory. The cost is the cost, however, and should not be tied to the cost of maintaining inventory. It should be tied to the budget of the department responsible for making the poor decision.

With shortage costs, many cost types are mentioned here, as well. They suggest that lost sales, loss of goodwill, overtime, customer dissatisfaction, and administrative costs are incurred. Loss of sales, goodwill, and dissatisfaction are all revenue issues. Overtime is a cost that might impact cash flow, as might certain administrative costs. One must be careful to not double count the administrative costs, however. The people performing the administrative tasks are covered under labor costs, and so there is no additional cost if, for example, an administrative worker must make extra calls to make up for inventory levels that are too low unless the call is long distance.

Finally, with order costs, most of the costs considered are costs that are covered by the resources that exist within the organization. It generally costs nothing to prepare and place an order unless there are specific transactional costs associated with two companies doing business, as might be the case with certain types of procurement exchanges. Otherwise, the organization is double counting if it tries to say that there is a cost for purchasing personnel to prepare a purchase order. The organization already pays the person to do his or her job, so why is there an additional cost?

What one should see is that managing inventory may not cost as much as one may be led to believe. The costs involved are the materials and the capacity associated with managing them; dedicated space, labor, equipment (e.g., storage and retrieval systems), and IT systems. "Dedicated," suggesting that if the inventory did not exist, the capacity necessary to manage the inventory would immediately go away, which paves the way for reduced costs.

The service level, therefore, has to take into account issues such as these to determine how much inventory is necessary and the costs involved in having it. There is not a single answer. The decision should be tied to specific issues such as the market, specific customers, products offered, competitive products being offered, the infrastructure required to manage the inventory, and so on.

Payables

Payables are generally much less involved than receivables. The organization should have an effective payables strategy that helps create a desirable working-capital position. This may mean that the organization can choose not to pay their bills exactly when invoiced but will pay them, so that they can get any discounts coming their way. Some organizations are in the habit of paying when they choose to pay and take the discount, whether deserved or not. The longer an organization can hold on to their cash, the better their cash flow will generally be. Extra days may mean increased nonoperating income if the cash is invested, which increases cash flow. Some organizations are so efficient that they can receive inventory, turn it into product, and receive payment for selling the product before they have to pay for the initial inventory. Their inventory and receivables are so small that they basically have negative working capital (see Equation 6.1). Organizations that can operate as effectively as this have the advantage of being able to invest money that they owe to others until it is due for payment.

THE SMALLER PLAYERS MAY HAVE TO MAKE ADJUSTMENTS TO THEIR OPERATIONS ELSEWHERE TO MAKE UP FOR THE POOR WORKING-CAPITAL POSITIONS.

By using cash flow–oriented measures, the organization can begin using its capacity decisions to understand how they impact cash flow. This is one of the first steps involved in aligning the organization with many of the cash flow measures associated with value-based management.

One point about payables strategies and overall working-capital strategies. Organizations that have tightly operating supply chains must figure out how to work together, so that one player does not dominate the capital in a supply chain. Organizations that position themselves to dictate payment terms and receipt terms are doing so to optimize their own position but may put others in a position where their working capital is less than desirable. The net effects of such a situation are that developing a truly collaborative partnership in a we–versus–them environment is very difficult to create.

How Does Capacity Impact Financial Dynamics?

Capacity has a major impact on financial dynamics because of the sheer amount of the company that it touches and influences. From a revenue perspective, it is the capacity of the organization to sell and deliver that often dictates its ability to generate revenues. From an expense perspective, a fair amount of the expenses that an organization incurs is tied to its space, labor, equipment, IT, and material capacity. Additionally, as these capacity entities begin to operate or function, they may incur action costs, which also increase the cost of operation. Finally, from a working-capital perspective, the capability of the processes and the competence of the capacity impacts the organization's ability to pay its bills, manage its inventory, and collect monies owed to the company. Production capacity and inventory management capacity may dictate how long capital is tied up in inventory.

The rest of this section will introduce some of the details about how capacity will impact the financial dynamics of the organization and how to make decisions that can improve financial measures through the utilization of capacity. Before doing so, the issue of productivity will be addressed here because it is important to understand what it really is and how it impacts capacity.

Productivity reflects the useful or value-adding work that capacity creates. "Useful" and "value-adding" should be considered in the context of the entity, operation, and process. For example, increasing production within a period of time by increasing the equipment processing rate, for example, may be a good thing for an operation. The entity is now able to process more in the same period of time, suggesting an increase in productivity. However, if the operation is not a constraining resource, overproduction, because there is excess capacity, does not improve the financial position of the firm (increase income, reduce working capital and expenses).

Doing so ties up capital and slows down the responsiveness of processes, as discussed in Chapter 7. Efficiently operating the non-constraining resource leads to a true understanding of the capacity level of operation which, in turn, may lead to the ability to reduce the capacity level. Improving and operating the constraining operation in a process to meet existing demand does add to the financial performance of the firm. The context for what is useful and value-adding began in Chapter 4 where the discussion centered on the purpose of processes and continued into Chapter 5 as one understands how operations come together to create processes. Each operation should have a role in the process, and productivity should be determined based on how the operation or the entity plays its role.

Increasing Capacity through Productivity Increases

Consider a salesperson who spends half of his or her time, or 20 hours, selling and half of his or her time doing paperwork. Doing the paperwork keeps him or her from being out in the field selling. Oftentimes, such paperwork is used for internal purposes only, leading to a situation where the salesperson is kept from selling because of internal requirements. The organization realizes this and wants to install a sales force automation software program to increase the productivity of its sales force. The argument is that the software will automate some of the paperwork and administrative tasks, leading to a lower cost of sales. Assume that the loaded rate for each sales person is $120,000 per year.

The justification for the software comes from the assumption that a 20% improvement in productivity will add up to $24,000 per sales person per year. For ten salespeople over three years, the savings are calculated as $720,000 in nondiscounted savings. For software costing $500,000, the deal made sense. The reality, however, is a different story. Making the salesperson more productive does not reduce the cost of sales. Increasing his or her productivity increases the amount of sales or value-adding work that he or she can perform in the same period of time (see Exhibit 6.4). Increasing productivity just increases the capacity to do value-adding work. Productivity increases increase the availability and/or the utilization of a resource. It does not reduce the cost of the resource. He or she still makes $120,000 per year. The only way that costs can go down is if this value was reduced or eliminated. Therefore, the organization spends $500,000 on anticipated savings of

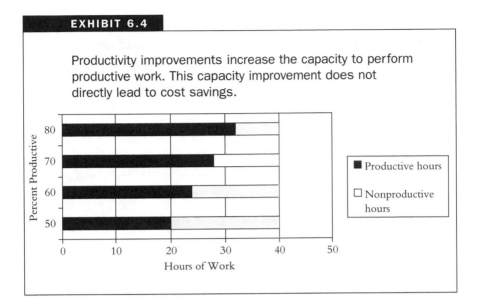

EXHIBIT 6.4

Productivity improvements increase the capacity to perform productive work. This capacity improvement does not directly lead to cost savings.

$720,000 and achieves no savings at all. From where will the financial improvements come?

Increasing Capacity Increases Action Degrees of Freedom

Such improvements to an organization create options. With improved productivity comes three options:

- Increase output
- Decrease input
- Do nothing

Output

Organizations that have increased the productivity of its sales force can attempt to improve financial performance by increasing output or sales. A 20% improvement in productivity translates into 4 hours per week or 200 hours per 50 week year. This is basically 5 extra weeks of selling each year. For someone with a $1 million-per-year quota, this benefit translates into the potential to sell approximately $100,000 more per salesperson per year, assuming that the demand exists to do so. It should not be assumed that this will just automatically happen, however. To achieve the benefit, the quotas must explicitly be increased to help ensure that the value is achieved.

Input

The organization has 10 salespeople. Assume that demand for the company's products was perfectly balanced with the output of the sales force, suggesting that the supply and demand were equal. With a 20% increase, each salesperson now has the capacity to perform 24 hours per week in value-adding activities each week. The total amount of value-added work capacity for the 10 people is now 240 hours per week. Only 200 hours are necessary. The labor capacity can now be reduced by 1 person, which equals $120,000 for one year. So, sales can remain the same and the $120,000 per year is saved. The net effect is that the organization now has 9 people working 24 hours of value-adding work, which is a total of 216 hours of capacity. Only 200 hours are needed. The organization must decide whether it wants to keep the extra worker. Eliminating another worker would increase the cost savings by $120,000 to a total of $240,000 per year. However, sales would drop off because the amount of value-adding hours is now 192. Recall, there is demand for 200 hours of work.

To decide what to do, the organization must consider the bottom-line impact of the decision. From a sales perspective, the organization is selling $10 million if each sales person just reaches quota. If each person has a sales quota of $20,000 per week, the output capability of 8 people is $160,000 per week and is $180,000 for 9 people. Although there is a $20,000 difference, the bottom-line impact of that is much smaller once margins are applied to the sales figures. The improvements must factor in the labor savings and the operational strategy to determine whether to keep the additional capacity or to cut it. Clearly, if the organization is in a growth mode or is expecting to be in a growth mode, it may want to keep the capacity. If it is in a reduction mode, it may want to reduce the capacity.

Do Nothing

An organization also has the option to do nothing. Doing nothing often happens by default when organizations believe that the improvements are automatically created by the solutions. Although it is commonly believed that an organization can buy a solution, implement it, and automatically receive the benefits, the reality of the situation is that there are often other activities necessary to create the improvements expected. Managers must understand how revenues are increased or how costs are decreased from a bottom-line perspective. When this is understood, the proper measures and metrics can be put into place to help ensure that some type of improvements occur. Additionally, sometimes tough decisions must be made. However, these decisions may be necessary if the organization wants to survive over the long run.

Achieving Value through Action

The way for organizations to achieve the identified value is to act on one or multiple degrees of freedom. To reduce costs, for example, the managers *must* eliminate the excess capacity from the organization that was created by the solution. If processes are being outsourced, the resources that used

TIPS & TECHNIQUES

There should never be a business plan or business case for cost reduction without a specific plan for identifying how the cost savings will occur. Saying that productivity goes up, therefore costs go down, is not enough.

to be necessary must be eliminated to achieve cost savings. Similarly, to achieve additional revenues, quotas must be increased to reflect the extra 5 weeks of value-adding work per year that the sales people can now perform. Identifying it and talking about it is not enough. The business case for the solution must address how explicit costs and explicit revenues are going to change and how the change will occur. This way, ambiguity regarding where cost savings will appear is completely eliminated and replaced with a specific plan to achieve value.

Revenues

There are limited ways to increase revenues. More products can be sold, which leads to more volume. The price of the products or services sold can be increased, leading to increased revenues. Or, one can choose to somehow do both. Properly managing the capacity of the organization is what will often help the organization to increase its revenues. The next sections will discuss how capacity can impact revenue increases.

Increasing Volume

Increasing revenues through increases in volume can come in one of two ways. First, the organization has increased its ability to meet existing demand, suggesting that the organizational processes were constraints. Second, the size of the demand is increased, leading to the potential use of more capacity to meet the demand. In the case of the former, the slowest operation, as discussed in Chapter 7, will constrain the ability to meet the demand that exists in the market. Managing the capacity of the constraint will help ensure that the organization is providing the maximum possible output.

Considering the latter, the organization has multiple options for helping to increase the size of the market. Increasing sales and marketing capacity might help identify or create additional demand. Additional

IT capacity may help organizations reach into areas of the world that are impossible to reach without it. Additional product development capacity might lead to an increase in market demand. Notice that the word *might* was used in all three cases. Just because the capacity exists does not mean that the market size will increase.

IN THE REAL WORLD

Strategic–Pricing Options

Often, organizations find themselves in a war of prices. If a competitor drops price, the question becomes what actions exist to help maintain at least the current level of financial performance. The authors of *How to Fight a Price War* offer their advice on how to handle the competitor who chooses to drop prices, and many of the solutions require efficient and effective capacity management.

Nonprice Responses

- Reveal your strategic intentions and capabilities, such as offering to match prices or revealing a cost advantage

- Compete on quality, which helps differentiate products

- Co-opt contributors, such as forming strategic and sometimes exclusive partnerships with or among key members of the demand chain

With these responses, the cost and quality capabilities are clear reflections of the amount and competence of the capacity in the organization. Managing to efficient and optimized processes can help lead to a low-cost structure. Process capability, capacity competence, and management competence will help lead the way toward high quality.

(CONTINUED)

Price Responses

- Use complex pricing actions, such as bundling the products or services or only changing certain prices

- Introducing new products that compete with the lower-priced products may offer some relief for organizations in a war

- Finally, organizations can just respond by lowering their costs[a]

   Similarly, the importance of capacity is clear. From a complex pricing perspective, the organization must be able to create the bundles through the management of material capacity and to create the products with its conversion processes. Introducing new products may require fast development processes that can reduce the costs involved in creating the new product. The last step is available to organizations who can take the financial hit. Increased tolerance is based on having the right infrastructure in place.

[a] Akshay R. Rao, Mark E. Bergen, and Scott Davis, "How to Fight a Price War," *Harvard Business Review*, 78, 2 (March–April 2000).

Increasing the market size requires the effective management of capacity. Putting up a web site to sell to a distant country without the delivery or support mechanisms in place will likely not lead to significant growth for certain types or products such as those found in abundance or cheaply in the new region. When determining whether to expand capacity and to what extent, a strong case must be made regarding what the expected outcome of the solution will be, and the outcome must improve business performance. Otherwise, the organization may end up increasing its capacity and, therefore, its expenses, without achieving revenue-based benefits required to improve overall performance.

Increasing Price

Increasing price often happens as a result of market conditions or through effective product- or service-planning. From a market perspective, issues such as supply and demand can impact the price of items and services sold. Lack of availability for some items can cause its price to increase. This is clearly not the case all of the time, and tactics that seek to take advantage of this must be carefully planned. Ultimately, an organization's ability to increase price on its own is partially a function of its competence to deliver that which supports the increased prices. This often involves introducing new products or services or uniquely combining products and services to create a more desirable product for the market. This requires highly competent capacity, such as product development, manufacturing, marketing, packaging, planning, or delivery, to all work together in a way that is unique to their respective firm and cannot be copied elsewhere. Capacity, therefore, impacts the organization's ability to identify and deliver strategies that allow the organization to increase price.

Costs

As suggested in the section on productivity, one may not achieve direct cost savings as a result of an improvement in capacity. Productivity increases *may* lead to reductions in the rate of increase of costs as demand grows. In other words, as demand for the capacity increases at some rate, the rate of increase of capacity may be some value less than the previous rate of increase. This may lead to increased margins. The improvement may or may not reduce costs, depending on the type of cost being considered and the amount of the capacity that exists. For example, capacity that is only 40% utilized at its maximum rate has 60% of its capacity still available. Assume that demand increases to the point that the maximum rate of utilization will now be 80% rather than the original 40%. Increases in productivity may allow the utilization rate to be 60% rather than 80%. So, the increased use of capacity is slower, but there is still only one resource required suggesting that the cost of the capacity is the same. The process may get more from the capacity in the form of output, but the input cost remains the same. Also, the point at which the organization must invest in more capacity may be extended. In such a situation, costs are not reduced, just postponed.

Organizations must seek the highest level of efficiency and effectiveness for its operations as possible. Efficient operation frees capacity. If there were no demand for the product of the process, costs can be cut, potentially, by reducing capacity. If there were not enough capacity, suggesting that the process is a constraint, efficient operations help the organization determine how much capacity is required and where it needs to be applied, so that demand can be met without incurring excessive amounts of expense.

When managing the cost of capacity, it will be important to understand the dynamics of capacity. A unit of capacity costs what it costs, suggesting a nonvariable behavior, and the objective is to have the right amount of resources to get the job done, whether planning for today or for the future. Although capacity is considered a resource cost, managing capacity effectively can lead to reductions in action costs, too. Capacity entities are organizational resource entities. Actions are the costs that are incurred as the capacity entities perform the tasks and activities necessary for them to do their jobs. Efficiently managing capacity, therefore, may also enable the organization to impact the rate of increase of action costs, as well. Costs are functions that increase monotonically. As one does more, costs will go up. However, the rate of cost increase for action costs can be impacted through effective capacity management. This, of course, can lead to improved margins. Organizations that plan effectively might be able to manage activities to explicitly ensure that the costs of the activities do not go up too quickly.

An example would be efficient and effective purchasing. Purchasing can be similar to shopping for items on sale. Buying bread that is $2.00 for two loaves costs more than one loaf of bread that costs $1.50. The issue is, what happens when demand is considered? If there is demand for two loaves of bread rather than one, buying the $2.00 bread is better than buying two loaves of the $1.50 bread at $3.00. Only at this point and beyond will it be better to buy the bread that is on sale. Why at two loaves and not before? Simply, because if someone buys two loaves and uses one, the cost was higher for the sales-priced bread. To achieve the benefits of purchasing, similarly, organizations must buy what it is going to use. With this criterion being a given, the efficient and effective management of purchasing can help identify similar benefits. Effective procurement processes are aware of inventory levels, demand patterns, and discounts to ensure that the ideal prices and quantities are procured. Orders can be combined for the right quantity discounts and to reduce the amount of capacity necessary to meet its demand.

Efficient and effective management of capacity can create benefits for organizations when the financial dynamics are understood. First, costs do not go down as one becomes more efficient. Efficiency can lead to a slower rate of cost increase for a given revenue growth level. The resulting benefit is increased margins from the fact that more output is being generated for a slower capacity increase rate. The ratio of output to input increases. Second, efficiency does not equal costs. It depends on the type of capacity, the amount of capacity, and the future demand requirements. Productivity increases lead to additional capacity, which creates options for the organization. The organization can choose to cut capacity, increase output, or to do nothing.

Working Capital

Capacity itself has less of a direct impact on working capital than it has for income and expenses, except when considering inventory. Unless the billing or collections departments are too small, for instance, it is not capacity per se that will determine the effectiveness of the process. It is the organizational strategy and the design and operation of the process that dictates the effectiveness of the process. With that being said, the organization will not want to carry too much capacity because this will negatively impact costs and, therefore, cash flow. The same holds true for payables. The right amount of capacity must be assembled and managed in a way that helps achieve desired service levels and financial performance.

Inventory, being capacity itself, has a significant impact on cash flow. As discussed previously, organizations must manage inventory effectively to demand levels to ensure that cash is not being tied up needlessly, therefore, creating a negative impact on cash flow.

Summary

Managing financial dynamics is both easier and more difficult than most people believe. It is more simple because costs always either remain the same or they go up unless their source is eliminated, so the emphasis should be on making the rate of increase slower during times of growth and to make the rate of elimination faster in times where markets and organizations are getting smaller. To achieve savings, the organization must understand the financial dynamics of their situation and understand the relationships between capacity management and financial dynamics management. Organizations often attempt to justify projects by suggesting that they will save money when, in fact, they do not and never will unless extraneous actions are taken.

The next chapter introduces the concept of optimization. It will take the concepts discussed previously and create an understanding of what it means to optimize a process, the impact on operations, and how to manage toward an optimal state.

Endnotes

[1] John D. Martin and J. William Petty, *Value-Based Management: The Corporate Response to the Shareholder Revolution* (Cambridge, M.A.: Harvard Business School Press, 2000).

[2] Reginald Tomas Yu-Lee, *Explicit Cost Dynamics: An Alternative to Activity-Based Costing* (New York: John Wiley & Sons, Inc., 2001).

[3] Reginald Tomas Yu-Lee, Hanno Lorenzl, "Broken Promises," *IIE Solutions* (October 2001).

[4] Reginald Tomas Yu-Lee, *Explicit Cost Dynamics: An Alternative to Activity-Based Costing* (New York: John Wiley & Sons, Inc., 2001).

[5] Elsayed A. Elsayed and Thomas O. Boucher, *Analysis and Control of Production Systems* (Englewood Cliffs, N.J.: Prentice-Hall, Inc., 1985).

[6] Ibid.

[7] Reginald Tomas Yu-Lee, *Explicit Cost Dynamics: An Alternative to Activity-Based Costing* (New York: John Wiley & Sons, Inc., 2001).

CHAPTER 7

Capacity Optimization

After reading this chapter, you will be able to:

- Define optimization and the components of an optimization problem
- Understand what optimization is not
- Discuss the benefits of optimization
- Understand how to optimize for operational performance
- Understand how to optimize for financial performance

Introduction

To this point in the book, the focus has been on identifying some of the essential and fundamental aspects of capacity management. The fundamental capacity components were defined in the earlier chapters. We discussed space, labor, equipment, IT, and materials as the building blocks for operations and processes. The key measures for each of the entities were identified, as well. The fundamental capacity measures were time, space, operations, and products. With the physical building blocks and the methods for measuring them defined, one can create any operation or process. Entities can be combined to create operations. A piece of equipment by itself, for instance, is basically useless. It usually needs materials, and possibly labor, to function. Hence, materials, labor, and equipment can combine to create an operation capable of processing or assembling parts. The measures are based on the result of combining the fundamental measures. A machine is capable of operating at a rate of W operations per unit of time. Labor is available for X hours per day. There are Y items in inventory available to create products. Each product requires Z inventory items. The process and product design determined the number of operations necessary to create each product. Each component or aspect is required to be known, so that an understanding of how much capacity exists at the operation can be created.

Bringing these measures together allowed us to define an operation. The output capability of the operation was determined by the output capabilities of the capacity (speed) and the inputs (time, materials, product/process design, and management information). Often the objective is to get the maximum output for a minimum or given level of input. So, the key output measure might be products per hour, but it might not make sense to achieve this output at any cost. You will try to manage the inputs effectively to have the least overall impact on the organization's finances and operations. The same holds true for a given input level. You will seek the greatest output from a given input level. Doing so requires effective planning and efficient utilization of the inputs. Material waste must be reduced. Time must not be lost due to poor operating and managing approaches. Tasks must be designed effectively to ensure a minimum of waste.

Operations and entities are combined to create processes. Processes involve the interaction of entities and operations to create some sort of output. Space (entity) holds the equipment, materials, and labor required to produce products. IT collects and stores the data required to manage the processes. It also can have the ability to process the data, so that managers have information that can help them manage the capacity more effectively.

The process dictates the desired output levels of the operations. A key criterion when designing or managing a process is managing its output levels and capabilities. With the output determined, the manager must look at the operations that make up the process and decide at what output levels each operation must operate to achieve the required level at the lowest level of input. Since the process sets the parameters for output levels of operations, you must focus on managing the process first, determine what is required of the operations, and determine measures and operating parameters for each operation. In other words, process trumps operation. Unfortunately, what often happens in organizations is that the operation trumps the process, resulting in poor decision-making. This is often the case when decision makers are overly focused on a particular operation, especially one that is considered somewhat expensive. Managers, in an attempt to ensure that expensive equipment is operating at its maximum, often create more than the desired amount of output to keep the operation running. This might often require feeder operations to operate at higher than necessary levels to feed the expensive machine. The net result is that the organization buys excess materials, pays for too much capacity, creates too much inventory, and ties its money up for too long, so that a fictitious cost can be minimized.

Once comfortable with the concept of managing a process, the levels of capacity and output that would achieve the objective best can be determined. By optimizing the process, the levels of inputs and outputs necessary to achieve the desired objective can be determined. For example, if the objective is to optimize revenues, the focus would be on figuring out how to get the most output, given the limits that may naturally or organizationally exist. The objective might be to focus on limiting or reducing costs given the demand, process, or organizational limits, which may exist that prohibit revenue growth. The objective may be to optimize working capital, again subject to the limitations, which may exist operationally, organizationally, or even contractually.

This chapter will take processes to this level. The desire is to help the reader understand the concept of optimization and its use. This is not meant to be a book on optimization. There are many books on optimization, optimization problems, and solution techniques that already exist. The objective is to introduce you to the concepts of optimization, so that you can begin to determine how optimization tools and techniques can be deployed to improve the management of your organization's capacity. This chapter will begin by defining optimization. It will discuss what optimization is and what the components of an optimization environment are. It will also discuss what optimization is not. The term *optimization* has become somewhat generic, leading to the misuse and misrepresentation of optimization. The chapter will provide some examples of various types of optimization problems to give the reader a flavor of how optimization works. This will be useful information for context building when applying optimization for your own organizations.

Defining Optimization

Optimization is a concept that involves modeling a situation and using techniques that are often math-based to find the *best* solution. Again, for emphasis, *optimization seeks the best solution.* The purpose of the emphasis is that *optimization* has been a term that has become overused almost to the point of becoming a cliché. During this process, important components of its definition have been lost. One often hears the term *optimization* being used when the term *improvement* is both connotatively and denotatively correct. The most abusive groups have been consultants, some software providers, and other service providers who talk about *optimizing* revenues, or *optimizing* costs, or *optimizing* purchasing. Not only are the terms used incorrectly, their meanings are often elusive, as well. Optimization is more than an improvement and should be used to reflect what it is: the best solution for a given objective and set of limiting factors or constraints. These constraints, discussed later in the chapter, simply keep the model from being able to improve indefinitely. For example, the fact that there are only 24 hours in a day, or a limited number of people available to produce products, or a limited number of people who can buy the products, among other issues, will keep that organization's revenues from increasing without bounds regardless of its product.

Optimization problems begin with an objective. This is the information or the solution parameter that the techniques will seek to optimize. The objective will often require that the solution *maximizes A* or *minimizes B*. For instance, the objective may be to maximize revenues or to maximize margins. It may be to minimize costs or minimize time. This is an objective statement that represents the prose form of an objective function. Every optimization problem must have an objective because it is the objective that defines the optimized solution. This should be apparent when considering the use of words such as *maximize* or *minimize*. Both are absolute terms that represent the optimization of the model. Only when the objective of maximizing revenues or minimizing costs is achieved can one say that they have reached an optimal state.

Optimization problems do not stop with objective statements or objective functions. The objective function is usually pretty simple to determine in prose form. Representing the objective is more difficult in its mathematical form. To reduce costs, there must be a realistic cost function. To improve revenues, there must be a realistic revenue function. It becomes more complicated when constraints are added.

With the objective defined and the constraints in place, the optimization problem begins to take its form. The objective may be to minimize costs, given that a certain level of output must be achieved. In other words, what is the cheapest way to make *X* widgets? One other example is to try to achieve the objective of maximizing revenues, given the fact that there are only *Y* people able to make products. In other words, how can we make the most money, given the fact that we only have Kim, Jim, and Tim working? Modeling the objective and the constraints must be defined very effectively, because any mistake or misrepresentation may have a major impact on the solution and its relevance.

Components of an Optimization Problem

A properly constructed optimization problem has certain features that help define it as such. Again, the optimization model seeks an optimal level and, therefore, certain components must exist. Those components are the objective function and the constraints. The objective function is then taken, the constraints are applied, and the problem is solved. Prior to implementing the solution, the results should be tested, implemented, and assumptions made in the model. It is a model and, therefore, some of the assumptions may or may not accurately reflect the actual operating model. Once the differences are reconciled, the problem can either be solved again with the new assumptions or the output can be adjusted to the output, based on the assumed impact of the modifications on the solution. Although the assumptions may change whether the solution remains optimal, the costs and benefits associated with seeking a truly optimal solution versus one that may be really close to optimal must be considered.

Objective Function

The objective function represents the prose objective mathematically. So, if the objective is to maximize the revenues of two products, A and B, that sell for \$12 and \$10, respectively, the objective function might be that found in Equation 7.1.

> **Optimize revenues = \$12 × A + \$10 × B, where A is the quantity of A sold and B is the quantity of B sold**
>
> *7.1*

In prose form, the objective might be to maximize the revenues of A and B, who have unit prices of \$12 and \$10, respectively.

It is of the utmost importance to model the objective properly. If the objective is improperly modeled, the objective will be achieved, but the solution will be meaningless.

Constraints

Constraints model that which limit the objective. Without constraints, the objective could continue on indefinitely. In a typical capacity problem, typical constraints may involve the fact that there is a limited amount of capacity and capacity availability. There might also be market-based constraints, such as minimum levels and maximum levels of demand. Consider the information contained in Exhibit 7.1. The two products have the following constraints. First, if there are 16 hours available for production, the total operating time on Operation 1 must be less than or equal to 16. The same holds true for Operation 2. Second, a minimum of 5 units of A must be produced and a minimum of 4 units of B must be produced. Operation 1, requiring the most processing time, is the constraint. The question becomes, given the constraints that exist, how much A should be made and how much B should be made to maximize revenues.

Solving the Problem

Solving the problem involves applying the constraints to the objective function. There are a significant number of solution techniques in existence, and they are beyond the scope of this book. The solution, therefore, is given in Exhibit 7.2. The optimal solution is to make 6 As and 23 Bs, even though As bring in the most revenue per part. The reasons are explained to the extent that it makes sense, given the scope of this book, later in the chapter, but it is this type of information and insight that an optimization problem can bring.

Testing the Solution

When determining the maximum solution, you will want to test the validity of the solution. Such testing may involve looking at the constraints again or the relative impact of the constraints on the real solution. What would happen, for example, if the organization alienated customers because it decided to significantly reduce production of product A from 10 to 5? Would this have an impact on those who wanted to buy Bs and who chose not to because As were not available?

EXHIBIT 7.1

Two products are represented with their processing time on each operation and the demand constraints.

Product	Time on operations 1 minutes	Time on operations 2 minutes	Minimum production units	Maximum production units
A	45	15	5	20
B	30	30	4	30

EXHIBIT 7.2

Maximum revenue occurs when 6 As and 23 Bs are made and sold.

Objective	Quantity of A	Quantity of B
$300	5	24
$302	6	23

You may also want to reassess the model to ensure that once implemented, all of the assumptions remain valid and the situation will, in fact, optimize performance.

Implementing the Solution

Finally, the organization must implement the solution. An open-loop implementation might involve implementation, and that is it: no follow-up or improvements to the system. However, it is highly recommended that you close the loop by assessing whether the solution had been obtained and if not, what can be improved to take the system toward a more desirable state. The organization will want to maintain its operations and seek to improve them by, perhaps, improving the operation time of the constraint. The feedback will be used to ensure that if the optimal values were not achieved, the organization understands this and works toward the optimal value by correcting what is currently wrong.

It is important to understand that the optimal solutions seek to optimize the current environment. When modeling today, you get the best answer for today. However, that does not mean that there is not a greater optimal state that one can achieve by redesigning and improving processes. This is a limitation of optimization models and the software that often uses them. The optimum output rate for a process may be 5 units per hour, but a better process may be capable of 10. Unless an optimal process to achieve the objective is sought, the solution will only address the static process and its constraints.

Examples of Optimization Problems

There are a large number of optimization problem types that exist. Each type has similar objectives and constraints and ultimately similar solutions. For the purpose of this book, only a few will be mentioned. The objective of listing them here is to give the reader some sense for the vast variety of problem types that exist for capacity management–related issues. The list is by no means exhaustive. It is an introductory list to give the reader an understanding of some of the fundamental problems that can be solved. Some of the more common capacity related problems are:

- *Blending:* determining what quantities of which materials to use
- *Product mix:* determining what products to make in what quantities to optimize the objective
- *Production planning:* determining how to minimize the inputs necessary to achieve a production plan or to meet demand
- *Logistics:* determining the best way to ship products so as to minimize costs and/or maximize customer service
- *Staffing:* determining what people should work when to achieve desired process output at minimum cost
- *Facility location:* locating facilities to minimize costs or time or to maximize delivery capability

An open mind should be kept while reading and understanding what is in each section. Ideally, the reader will be able to classify some of his or her processes or capacity management–related decision-making scenarios into this or similar categories. You may even need to create new types of problems. This list will help you to begin thinking about the models themselves, the objectives, and what might constrain the objective. As you begin to think about your own processes, the concept of the objective and the constraints should become clear in your mind.

What Optimization Is Not: A Plea for Being Correct

As discussed earlier, optimization is about seeking the best solution. The best solution will refer to an optimal solution that occurs when something is maximized or minimized. When not used in this context, the meaning of the concept and the philosophy of optimization are lost.

TIPS & TECHNIQUES

Simulation programs provide an excellent way to determine whether the optimal state performs as anticipated. By modeling and piloting the process, assumptions can be tested and exposed, leading to the potential to avoid solutions built on poorly modeled reality and for developing better future models.

When lost, optimization can come to mean practically anything and, therefore, becomes useless to an organization. When considering optimizing your organization, the first issue to consider is, what is the objective? Is the objective to optimize the process for accounts receivable so that the cost is at a minimum? Is it to maximize revenues? Is it to minimize the cycle time of the overall process? The second issue is to begin thinking about what constrains the organization from reaching an optimal state now. Policies, procedures, customers, time, technology: all of these issues can come into play when trying to optimize the process. The third is to go through the rigor to achieve the optimized solution. This can be done by hand or using computers. Conceptually, it does not matter. What does matter is that the process has been modeled and solved accurately, leading to solutions that have meaning for the organization. If these steps are not followed, it is not likely that the process has been optimized.

Benefits of Optimization

The next question to be answered is why organizations look to optimize operations. The answer is simply that there are significant benefits associated with processes that have achieved an optimal state. The first benefit is that optimization can help organizations achieve desired operational performance. Operational performance focuses on how effectively the organization's operations achieve its objectives. So, if the objective is to maximize output, optimization solutions can define the solution that will help ensure the solution. If the objective is to minimize overall lead time or cycle-time, optimization solutions will provide the necessary information for managers to reduce the values to their optimal levels.

The second benefit is that optimization can help achieve maximum levels of financial performance. With financial performance being the focus, you can begin to define problems or solution environments where the parameters that are being measured lead to increased profitability and cash flow. Choosing to optimize revenues will lead to solutions where the techniques will apply the constraints to the system and determine the greatest amount of revenue that can be achieved. Many times, the solutions are counterintuitive because many parameters come together in ways that are not always anticipated. For example, revenues and time requirements and time constraints can come together in a way that higher revenue items with longer processing times are not produced in favor of lower revenue items that have a slower processing time. Cost optimization alone is dangerous because there must be an effective cost function, and there should be minimum output requirements or expectations. An improper cost function will not lead to solutions that optimize the real cost situation. Not having minimum expectations and/or a proper cost function leaves the door open for the extreme cost minimization, which could ultimately be that costs are zero.

Finally, an organization can seek to optimize both operational and financial performance. By properly defining the objective function and the constraints, many techniques exist that will enable organizations to achieve their goals. Although the techniques themselves may be beyond the scope of this book, some of the concepts associated with solving these problems will be discussed in the next section. When carefully used, such techniques can begin to reveal information about the process and the model that will help managers improve their operations.

Optimizing from an Operational Performance Perspective

Desired operational performance involves seeking the best solution from either an input management perspective or an output management perspective. Described this way, the emphasis is placed on the operation itself and the aspects necessary to manage it rather than the financial implication of doing so. What is the difference? From an input management perspective, the objective is to minimize the input capacity entities and operations for many reasons. With space limitations, the objective is to use the least amount of space. With budget constraints, one may choose to rid the department of resources rather than keep them. How an organization utilizes its budget may not have an impact on cash flow—depending on how the money is being spent. From an output perspective, the objective may be to make the greatest number of parts subject to demand constraints.

The next sections will begin to discuss operational optimization in a bit more detail. The reader is encouraged to read the sections and consider how they manage and may improve their operations.

Input Optimization

Input optimization involves creating a desired level of output with the minimum amount of inputs. The inputs under consideration are the capacity entities of space, labor, equipment, IT, and materials. Again, input minimization does not necessarily translate into costs or cost savings. The desire is to ensure that the minimum number and level of entities are involved in achieving the output level under consideration. Why this may not translate into cost savings depends on the specific situation. For example, if an organization owns space, saving space may not impact the cash flow of the situation. The space may either be paid for or the payments are pre-determined and independent of how the space is being utilized. An organization may want to preserve its labor capacity by minimizing the use of labor resources on certain processes. Labor costs may not go down because the people are still being paid at the same rate. Therefore, there are ways that inputs can be minimized without the solution being translated into direct cost savings.

Capacity Entities

The next section will discuss the capacity entities briefly. Recall from Chapter 3, each of the entities was introduced with the respective key operating parameters. The purpose is not to create an exhaustive list but to introduce you to some of the key parameters for you to consider as you begin to understand what you can and cannot control. It can also be used as the basis for improvement or for improvement efforts. Each entity is discussed in turn.

Space

Space is measured in spatial measures such as square feet or cubic meters (Exhibit 7.3). When optimizing with space as a parameter, the availability of the space might be an issue, as well. If, for example, there is not 24-hour security of some sort or if there is another limiting factor (such

---

EXHIBIT 7.3

Space with the key measures and constraints to its improvement.

Entity	Key Measures	Key Constraints
Space	• Area/volume	• Total area
	• Examples ft², ft³, m², m³	• Area available for operations
	• Time	• Time availability

EXHIBIT 7.4

Labor with the key measures and constraints to its improvement.

Entity	Key Measures	Key Constraints
Labor	• Time	• Available time
	• Hours, minutes,seconds	• Maximum
	• Operating rate	operating rate
	• Units/hour	• Space allowed
	• Units/minute	per person
	• Tasks/hour	
	• Tasks/minute	
	• Space	

---

as a lack of lights on a softball field that one might schedule) and people do not have access to space, this may have an impact on outputs. When looking to minimize space as an input, there may be a maximum limit on the amount of space that can be taken up. For example, total space must be less than or equal to the maximum space available. The idea would be that whatever occurs, it must be limited to the existing space.

Labor

The key measures for labor are time, operating rate, and space (see Exhibit 7.4). Time is critical because the availability of labor resources is primarily defined in terms of time. When minimizing input, therefore, there will be maximum available time constraints. One may want to limit workers to a 10-hour shift, and can even provide mathematical penalties in the model for exceeding the 10 hours. Operating rate is something that either results from the circumstances or is managed. It naturally occurs when the competence of the labor resources is considered. Some people are just faster or slower than others. It can be managed with equipment, as managers seek to limit the speed at which the labor/equipment operation is operating. Finally, space requirements are important. One may choose to limit the amount of space that is allocated to each individual. This, too, will help minimize the inputs to a process.

Equipment

Equipment is often a key component when seeking an optimization solution. It has natural limits that provide constraints whether managers want them, or not. The key measures, found in Exhibit 7.5, are time, operating rate, and space. As with labor, time and operating rate are important measures because they will dictate the output. Time can be limited by factors such as labor or materials since the equipment can basically be considered perpetually available. Operating rate is bounded by natural upper limits, but managers can also choose to operate the equipment at a slower rate. This is akin to driving a car with a top speed of 150 miles per hour at 70 miles per hour. There is nothing wrong with managing this way.

If available space and equipment both exist or are both predetermined, this may constrain output. Equipment with similar capabilities but different sizes may be moved around and rearranged, but for the most part,

EXHIBIT 7.5

Equipment with the key measures and constraints to its improvement.

Entity	Key Measures	Key Constraints
Equipment	• Time	• Available time
	• Operating rate	• Operating rate
	• Units/hour, hours/unit	
	• Units/minute, minute/hour	
	• Tasks/hour, hours/task	
	• Tasks/minute, minutes/task	

EXHIBIT 7.6

Information technology with its key measures and constraints to its improvement.

Entity	Key Measures	Key Constraints
IT	• Cycle-time, instructions/second, floating point operations/second, vectors/second, bits per second, cycles per second • Time • Storage	• System speed capabilities including processor, graphics, I/O • Available time • Available memory/storage space

you have what you have. When purchasing equipment, you will have more flexibility over minimizing spatial requirements of the new equipment.

Information Technology

The extent to which IT impacts processes depends greatly on the process itself. Where processes are dependent on IT, such as with document creation, product design, video and graphics, highly transactional environments, and research, IT takes on a role similar to that of more traditional equipment. The capacity and speed of IT become critical measures and potentially significant constraints (see Exhibit 7.6). Speed in this case represents the total speed capability of the system and not just the processor speed or the graphics speed. With processes that require, but may not be limited to, the IT abilities of the organization, the speed is not critical, as long as there is enough. You do not often see accounts receivable bogged down because of slow processor speed. Although it can happen, especially with small companies that may be running off of a PC or small office computer, it is not the norm.

Another important measure is availability. No matter how fast or slow the computers are, if they are not available, they will not be able to provide process support. If computer availability requires labor support, you can plan availability. The organization might want to limit unplanned availability shortages, however.

Materials

Materials, as with the other capacity inputs, can be limited without necessarily having a financial impact. For example, with a limited amount of raw materials, the objective may be to limit the amount of the material that goes into noncritical or less profitable products. The two key measures for materials are the number of units available and the space that each unit requires (see Exhibit 7.7). Units available clearly limits output and may also limit processing time. Space may become an issue when it is limited and would, therefore, limit the number of units that can be stored. In other words, limited space impacts the size of the inventory (units available).

Output Optimization

Output optimization focuses on the processing and delivery components of a process. The objective is to optimize that which is involved with creating products at a rapid rate and/or reducing the total amount of time necessary to do so. From this perspective, there are two key measures that must be emphasized:

EXHIBIT 7.7

Materials with the key measures and constraints to their improvement.

Entity	Key Measures	Key Constraints
Materials	• Units	• Units available
	• Space	

- Throughput
- Lead time

Throughput represents the rate of products being made and is generally measured as parts leaving the system per unit of time. Lead time represents the amount of time that a product spends in the process waiting to be completed. The lead time is generally measured from when the product enters the process in its earliest form and ends as it exits the process. Throughput and lead time are not one and the same. Short lead time is not necessarily equal to high throughput. Additionally, long lead times do not necessarily equal low throughput.

Maximum throughput will occur when the process is operating at its maximum rate. This does not presuppose that each operation is at its maximum, only the process. The slowest operation or the constraint determines the maximum possible rate. The operating rate of the constraint, by definition, dictates the maximum throughput that process is capable of, and the process will achieve this rate, so long as the operations downstream from the constraint do not negatively impact the flow of materials or information and the upstream operations do not starve the constraint of parts. If a constraint resource is only capable of processing 5 units per hour while the other operations are capable of processing more, the maximum output will be limited to 5 units per hour. The maximum rate of a process is only achievable when the constraint is operating at full capacity. If the constraint is operating at anything less than what it is fully capable of, the maximum throughput of the entire process will be limited to the rate at which the constraint is operating.

In the example above, therefore, if the constraint is operating at a value of 3 units per hour rather than 5, the maximum throughput of the process given this operating rate is 3 units per hour. This may or may not be bad. If there were demand for 4 or more units, the low utilization rate or operating rate could keep the organization from receiving revenues of up to 2 units per hour if the process output units were to be sold. If the process output were invoices, and if the average invoice were for $100,000, the constraint causes an additional $1.6 million (2 fewer invoices each hour leads to 16 fewer invoices per in-cash each day at $100,000 per invoice) to be tied up because it pushes the invoice and therefore the collection of the cash out into the future.

When operating at maximum capacity, the throughput and lead time are independent. This is because the constraint dominates the output and the lead time is determined by where one is in the waiting line, or queue. Think of a car wash on a beautiful Saturday morning. If you get there before anyone else does, the lead time is pretty short. The car wash is operating at a rate where the constraint is the market demand. If the demand existed, the process would become the constraint and the lines would begin to increase. Not everyone in line has the same wait time. The length of the line dictates the anticipated lead time. The car washers can operate at their maximum throughput rate, but they just cannot process fast enough. The independence, therefore, exists because one variable does not predict the other: there is not necessarily a simple function that predicts exactly one variable when given the other, unless all variables are kept constant, which is an unrealistic expectation. For example, a long queue will not predict a varying operating rate. One can have a 10-minute wait because of a slow operating rate or because they are in line. A three-cars-per-hour output can have queues that are as long as those for a five-cars-per-hour output.

The next two sections will describe throughput and lead time in more detail. The objective is to begin discussing the issues that should be addressed when considering the optimization of either one. Similar to outputs, the key measures will be discussed along with that which constrains the process from achieving the measure.

Throughput

What Is Throughput?

As described above, throughput here represents the output rate of a process. It can only be measured by determining how much of a product comes out of the end of the process over time. Doing so takes into account interactions between operations that occur upstream. This is an important distinction because you may know the exact output rate of an operation, but as operations interact, many influencing factors may prevent the maximum theoretical output from being achieved.

Throughput should be measured in output per unit time, or output/time. Examples include parts/hour in the case of a manufacturing process. It may include invoices/hour if measuring a receivables process or check/hour if measuring a payables process. Regardless of the type of process, measuring its output over time will give a feeling for the capabilities of the process or, potentially, the level of demand that may exist. When seeking to optimize throughput, one will attempt to maximize (versus minimize) the throughput of the process rather than the throughput of the individual operations, except for the case where the operation is a constraint. Clearly, this will involve trying to determine the maximum output rate of the process, which involves coming as close to the output rate of the constraint as possible.

Whether products, checks, or reports, throughput is the key output, or results-oriented process measure. Throughput will also dictate the parameters for how capacity should support the process. Beginning with the throughput values, one can analyze the process and determine what capacity at what availability and utilization is necessary to achieve the desired throughput.

Measuring and Influencing Throughput

Measuring the throughput of a process in its most simple form requires determining the output rate of the process. Output is measured in units. The problem with measuring only output is that it tells very little about the operating rate of the process. Not having this information does little in terms of helping one manage capacity. If output were 100 units, for example, would this represent 100 units per day? One hundred per week? Month? Year? The basic capacity necessary to produce 100 units may be relatively constant, but how much of the capacity is needed when time varies? The capacity to create 100 units today is configured differently than if the same output were needed over a three-month period. The output rate, which is output ÷ time, determines throughput. When considered in this perspective, throughput is the first derivative of output.[1]

Since optimizing throughput involves seeking the maximum throughput rate, it suggests analyzing the process and trying to figure out the maximum rate that the process can achieve. From our knowledge to this point, we know that the maximum throughput is deter-

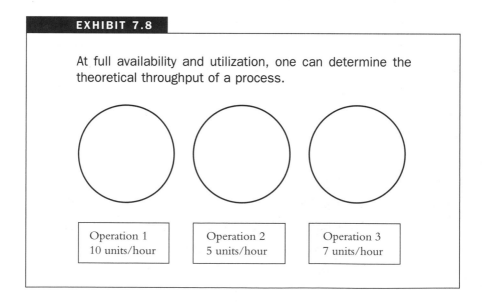

EXHIBIT 7.8

At full availability and utilization, one can determine the theoretical throughput of a process.

| Operation 1 | Operation 2 | Operation 3 |
| 10 units/hour | 5 units/hour | 7 units/hour |

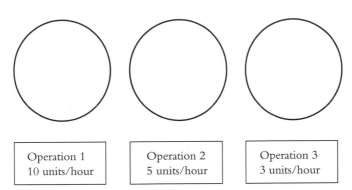

EXHIBIT 7.9

Poor availability/utilization versus process constraint.

Operation 1	Operation 2	Operation 3
10 units/hour	5 units/hour	3 units/hour

With the availability of Operation 3 at 42%, its output rate declines from seven units per hour to three. Poor availability and/or utilization can cause an operation with more than enough throughput capability to become a process constraint.

mined by the constraint. The process will not be able to operate at a rate faster than that dictated by the constraint. The process can, however, operate at rates slower than the constraint. Downstream operations may prohibit the process from achieving what it is capable of achieving, even if the constraint is operating at maximum levels. Consider the process represented in Exhibit 7.8. The process has a maximum throughput potential of 5 units per hour. This maximum level is dictated by the constraint. However, low utilization or availability of the third operation can actually cause the third operation to become the constraint (see Exhibit 7.9). Even though the process is theoretically faster, there is something that causes it to operate in a manner that robs itself of throughput. What robs the process is the downtime of the operation, often created by ineffective capacity management.

Effective capacity management, when seeking to optimize throughput for an existing process, is impacted by three things:

- Time and availability
- Operating rate
- Capacity levels

Time, Availability, Utilization

When managing a process such as that represented in Exhibit 7.8, the availability and utilization of the resource must be effectively managed. When maximizing throughput, the objective is to get the most out of the process. You can only get 5 units per hour from the process in this configuration. Therefore, the organization must do what it can to ensure that the 5 units per hour are achieved, assuming demand exists for the products.

The organization must make its decisions considering whether there are financial objectives that must be met or not. When managing the process without a financial objective, the capacity of Operations 1 and 3 would not be an issue. Additionally, it does not matter how long capital is tied up in inventory when considering a manufacturing operation. In this case, one may attempt to keep availability and utilization levels as high as possible. Operation 1 can operate at double the rate of Operation 2 and will, therefore, ensure that Operation 2 continues running. Ensuring that Operation 2 is running is a good thing. Building up capacity between the two operations is not. As discussed in the next section on lead time, if the product is a manufactured item, the inventory being created is the enemy of lead time. In a situation such as this, the average amount of time that a piece of inventory remains in queue increases. This means that the amount of time that the organization's capital is tied up, too, increases, which has a negative impact on cash flow.

Another issue that the organization must address is the fact that, Operation 2 impacts the level of utilization that can be maintained by Operation 3. Operation 3 is faster, so it will become starved for work. If the utilization of Operation 3 is measured and management seeks to maximize it, they will be continually disappointed because a slower process is feeding it.

When managing with both throughput and financial objectives, the solution becomes quite different. The emphasis shifts to getting the maximum throughput while minimizing capacity. To accomplish this, you must try to figure out what availability levels are necessary and then determine the required utilization levels. Why availability? Simple. Availability is tied more directly to fundamental capacity levels. When measuring the throughput of an operation by beginning with the availability of the process, you gain an understanding of whether the base capacity of the operation is sufficient. If the operation is at maximum availability, you look to the utilization. If the utilization is not where it should be, there is a management problem that needs to be addressed. If the utilization is at its maximum levels, management must do three things. First, it must increase the output of the process to make sure that the process can meet the demand. Second, it must reassess the capabilities of the process and update the information used for management purposes. Finally, it may act to increase capacity by increasing the operating rate, covered next, by improving the competence of the operation (units/time) or by increasing capacity homogeneously by adding more capacity of the same type.

If the improvement were to begin with utilization first, one may spend significant resources trying to improve utilization and find out that the constraint is ultimately the availability of the operation. A machine that is available for 50% of the time will make efforts to improve utilization from 50% to 80% seem worthless. The constraint is the availability, and fixing it will provide much more information for management purposes than if one were to arbitrarily improve utilization.

With both cases considered, operating with and without financial objectives, the manager now has the fundamental information necessary to optimize throughput. With the existence of a process constraint comes the assumption that demand exceeds the capability of the process. In other words, in our example, the demand would be for 6 units per hour, or above. If the demand were for 4, the process's ability to operate at 5 units per hour should suggest that the process itself is not a constraint. When demand exceeds the ability of supply to meet it, one does the following.

- Answer the following question: Is the constraint operating at full capacity? Determine the availability and utilization levels and ensure that they are at maximum levels. Often, poor upstream scheduling or decisions, in addition to not ensuring that the constraint is operating at its maximum levels, can impact the throughput of the constraint. At one company, for example, a worker took it upon himself to minimize set-up at his nonconstraint operation by combining batches. He was praised for his work. However, the action killed the utilization of the heat-treat, which was a constraint operation, because the sequence of materials that would maximize the utilization at the constraint was disrupted. He saved time at an operation that did not need it and harmed the total throughput of the process.

- If the constraint is at its maximum levels, are poor availability and/or poor utilization creating downstream constraints? If this is the case, you must identify where the constraint exists and improve its availability, its utilization, or both, so that it does not impede throughput. Managers should focus on the throughput of the process and the measures should support the throughput of the process. This will expose improperly managed operations, and managers can then improve the processes to ensure that ideal throughput levels are obtained.

Operating Rate

Increasing the operating rate of an operation can provide excess capacity whether the operation is a constraint or not. The operating rate is equal to the throughput of an operation (see Equation 7.2). The throughput of the operation is determined by the speed of the operation itself, the design of that being processed, the design of the operation, and the competence of those responsible for managing the operation.

$$\frac{\text{parts}}{\text{hour}} = \frac{\text{parts}}{\text{operations}} \times \frac{\text{operations}}{\text{time}} \qquad 7.2$$

Improving Parts/Operation

As discussed in Chapter 3, the ratio of parts per operation is determined by the design being processed and by the operation. Assume that there is a fixed value at which the operation operates and assume that this value is 100 operations per hour. Assume further that the parts operation ratio is 1 part/10 operations. That translates into a capacity of 10 parts/hour. Assume now that the organization requires a capacity level equal to 12 parts/hour. The only way to achieve this level is to reduce the number of operations per part to a value of eight or less. In other words, at eight operations per part, the process is capable of producing approximately 12.5 units/hour.

There are a number of techniques available that managers can use to improve the parts/operations ratio. Traditional industrial engineering techniques, such as value engineering and design for manufacturability, can be used to figure out how to improve the throughput. These techniques can focus on ensuring, for example, that every step in the process adds value and is as simple to manufacture as possible. They may also focus on determining whether steps can be combined, therefore requiring fewer operations to perform a task.

Improving the competence of the labor component of the operations can also improve the ratio. Oftentimes, more competent workers can determine valid ways to accomplish the same work with fewer steps. If this happens, the organization can emphasize the importance of such improvements by testing the solution and incorporating it into the process.

Trying to improve the operation/time ratio is a bit more tricky under most normal circumstances. First, one may want to know whether the process is operating at its maximum sustainable output rate. If not, the objective may be to increase it. This next solution is obvious but often overlooked, believe it or not. Second, organizations may work to increase capacity by buying additional equipment to supplement the current equipment or replace the current equipment with newer and faster equipment (that is, a homogeneous capacity increase). The decision to do so depends, again, on whether there is a financial component. If there are no financial objectives or constraints, one can just purchase equipment based on constraints such as space. If there are financial issues, however, the problem becomes more complicated.

Consider the process in Exhibit 7.6. Assume that the 5 units per hour is determined by Equation 7.3.

$$\frac{5 \text{ units}}{\text{hour}} = \frac{100 \text{ operations}}{\text{hour}} \times \frac{1 \text{ part}}{20 \text{ operations}} \qquad 7.3$$

Assume that the operations are to either double capacity by purchasing another of the same type of equipment or to buy a faster piece of equipment. The new equipment is 50% faster than the existing equipment. There are a number of issues to consider when doing the financial justification for the purchase. First, the maximum throughput that can be achieved if Operation 2 is increased beyond 7 units per hour is 7 units per hour. With the capacity of Operation 2 exceeding 7 units per hour, the only revenue increase possible is the increase from 5 to 7.

Above 7 units, Operation 3 is the constraint. Hence, investing in the option where one significantly increases the capacity should be made with two issues in mind. First, what do you get in the short term? The financial justifications must consider current expectations, which would only allow that revenues would increase by the 2 units per hour gained from the increase. The second is, will the capacity be utilized at some time in the future? If the demand continues to grow and capacity will be increased in some cases, it might make sense to invest in the capacity now. You must be assured that the technology will not become obsolete prior to getting to this point.

By selecting the faster equipment (7.5 units per hour) and replacing the older equipment, the organization does not have significant excess capacity. Operation 3 would become the constraint but only until its capacity is slightly increased.

With the doubling, the organization is capable of operating at a rate of 3 units per hour above the constraint operation. A positive aspect of having excess capacity is the ability of the capacity to ensure that the constraint is constantly operational. If the operations are close in capacity, it is more likely that there will be increased downtime for the constraint than when there is sufficient capacity. This is due to the fact that with large capacity differences, the equipment can overcome low availability or utilization. If down for 3 hours, for example, the doubled capacity can make up for downtime by producing at a much faster rate than the constraint. Slower equipment will make up the difference at a much slower rate. This difference can be important if downtime is a regular occurrence, as the constraint may be in jeopardy of being starved for parts.

In solutions like this, the business case is likely to be incorrect because the revenue projections are often improperly calculated. To model the business case effectively, one might need to assume lower output rate or get a more accurate output rate by simulating the process in software.

There are other considerations, as well, when making investments to maximize throughput. The decisions center on what the future expectations of throughput are and also on planned investments in improving capacity levels. Considering demand, for instance, if demand is expected to increase substantially, you may make the investment now because it will be utilized at a point in time in the future. Additionally, if it is expected that management is going to increase the capacity of the third operation it may only be a constraint for a limited amount of time. It might make sense, therefore, to invest in the excess capacity.

Summarizing, when optimizing throughput, the objective is to focus on the constraints. The constraint must operate at a rate that is equal to the maximum degree that is practical. The potential to increase the throughput of the constraint may also be an option. Increasing the capacity of resources that are not constraints will not produce an overall increase in throughput unless the poor management of the operations cause it to become the constraint.

Lead Time Optimization

Excessive lead time is frustrating to organizations. Oftentimes, they are operating at maximum throughput rates, yet lead times are much too long. The question is, why? Lead time is a function of the amount of time an item must wait to be processed and the processing time itself. The processing time will often remain the same. So, if an order takes a significant amount of time longer, it is likely due to increased waiting time.

Assume that an item arrives at a two-step process. If there are no items waiting to be processed on the first operation, it can begin processing right away. Once finished with the processing, it proceeds to the next operation. Assume no transportation time for now. If there are no products waiting to be processed at the second operation, it is immediately processed. The total lead time is just the processing time for the item.

Assume now that the item arrives at the first operation and there are other parts waiting to be processed. Let us say that it must wait 15 minutes to be processed. Once processed, it proceeds to Operation 2 again with no transportation time. At Operation 2, there is no wait time. The total lead time has increased by 15 minutes. If the part incurs transportation time and additional wait time at Operation 2, the lead time will increase by the amount of wait and transportation time.

To minimize lead time, the time that the part must wait to be processed must be reduced or eliminated. There are three main culprits for increased wait time.[2]

- Inventory
- Suboptimal scheduling
- Suboptimal process layout and operations

Inventory

Inventory is the enemy of lead time. The more inventory that is in the system, the more that must be processed. Any particular part must wait for the others in front of it to be processed. The more inventory that must be processed, the greater the processing time. Unfortunately, organizations tend to process large amounts or in large batches and that creates a scenario that, although the throughput may be optimized, it takes the customer forever to get its products. This creates a negative customer satisfaction.

Organizations must do all that they can to reduce inventory. In the absence of financial objectives, the excessive inventory increases wait time. With financial objectives, the excessive inventory leads to excessive lead time, which ties up capital for a much longer period and increases the potential for the inventory to become obsolete. Capital being tied up reduces the cash flow revenue potential that results from investing the capital. Obsolete inventory leads to losses of money and time.

Suboptimal Scheduling

Suboptimally scheduling operations within a process can lead to increased lead time. Arbitrarily scheduling work on machines, for instance, may increase the lead time of items in the system. Consider the scenario defined in Exhibit 7.10. There are three orders that need to be processed on two operations. Assume that the average lead time is determined by dividing the total processing time of the three orders by 3. Operation 2 is the constraint operation. Once the first order is completed on Operation 1, it will go to Operation 2. When the second order is processed, it must wait for the first one to be finished on the second operation. Once the first order is finished on Operation 2, the second can begin immediately. In other words, Operation 2 will operate continually (see Exhibit 7.11).

EXHIBIT 7.10

Improvements to processes should consider tactical and strategic issues.

Option	Capacity	Issues
Double with same equipment	200 operations/hour 10 parts/hour	• Operation 3 becomes constraint. Throughput is limited to 7 units/hour
Replace with faster equipment	150 operations/hour 7.5 parts/hour	• Cost benefit must consider the impacts of new equipment on throughput

---

EXHIBIT 7.11

Three orders with their processing times.

	Processing time on Operation 1	Processing time on Operation 2
Order 1	15	35
Order 2	18	40
Order 3	21	50

EXHIBIT 7.12

Sequence of the order has an impact on throughput time and, therefore, average lead time.

Sequence	Total Lead time	Average Lead time
1–2–3	120 minutes	40 minutes
1–3–2	120 minutes	40 minutes
2–1–3	123 minutes	41 minutes
2–3–1	123 minutes	41 minutes
3–1–2	126 minutes	42 minutes
3–2–1	126 minutes	42 minutes

In this case, changing the order of the orders may seemingly not make a difference. It does, however, and here is why. The processing time on the constraint will always be the same: 105 minutes. Nothing can be done to change this. To reduce the total time, we would start the 105-minute activity as early as possible. As seen in Exhibit 7.12, the shortest total processing time and, therefore, the lowest lead time occurs when order 1 is first.

With order 1 first, the constraint is started as quickly as possible. When order 1 is first, the constraint begins its 105 minutes in 15 minutes. With order 2, it starts 3 minutes later and with order 3, a full 6 minutes later. There are a number of techniques, such as Johnson's rule, that show how to optimally sequence orders to minimize lead time and they should be considered when seeking to minimize lead time.[3]

Process Layout

The final issue considered is the layout of the process. Layouts requiring excessive transit time also potentially increase the overall wait time. Any time spent going from one location to another is time spent in a manner that is not leading to the product being created. The only time that transportation will not increase wait time is if the queue for the next process is larger than the transportation time. For example, an operation that has a 10-minute queue in front of it will not experience the 5-minute transit time for materials coming from the previous operation. This, however, is no excuse for poor process design. First, transportation time may become a constraint if inventory levels are reduced. Second, even if inventory levels are not reduced, the organization must maintain transportation capacity. This capacity may not add to the product being made or enhanced, suggesting that the capacity adds cost without adding value to the process.

This, of course, has a negative impact on the organization's profitability. There are times when transportation adds value. With a specific product that has limited availability or very large size, one may charge for the delivery of the product. Additionally, organizations that ensure fast delivery may add value, as well. It depends on the situation. I have been guilty of asking someone to FedEx something that I did not quickly review. The result was money being spent for a fast delivery when I did not really need such turnaround. In cases like this where there is fast turnaround but the product still sits in queue, one must question whether value has been added or not.

Lead time reduction is often a very difficult proposition, but as long as managers focus on the topics discussed in this section, their lead time performance will improve. The objective is to look to reduce lead time through reduced inventory levels, more effective scheduling and sequencing, and better process layouts.

This concludes the operational component of optimization. The emphasis has been on optimizing an operating measure. The first was throughput and the objective was to maximize the throughput value. The second was to optimize lead time. The objective here is to minimize throughput. The subject is now going to shift away from optimizing operations toward optimizing the financial component of the process.

IN THE REAL WORLD

Finding the Hidden Reasons for Process Success

The Toyota Production System has been studied and copied by many manufacturing organizations throughout the world, yet few can emulate its success. Part of the reason that its success cannot be emulated is based on the fact that the observers are looking for, and at, the wrong causes. Steven Spear and H. Kent Bowen studied the Toyota Production System and reported their findings in their article, "Decoding the DNA of the Toyota Production System." In their work, the authors found that the rules and approaches that are in place basically allow for process and operation self-improvement. This is done via the scientific method and four rules that help ingrain the approach into the workers. The rules are:

- All work must be highly specified as to content, sequence, timing, and outcome.

- Every customer-supplier connection must be direct, and there must be an unambiguous yes-or-no way to send requests and receive responses.

- The pathway for every product and service must be simple and direct.

- Any improvement must be made in accordance with the scientific method, under the guidance of a teacher, at the lowest possible level in the organization.[a]

When considered from a capacity management perspective, one finds an unending desire to always improve and simplify the process. By specifically planning the rules and relationships, processes and operations interact much more effectively and efficiently, leading to minimal excess capacity, a high degree of flexibility, and highly competent processes and operations.

(CONTINUED)

Optimizing Financial Dynamics

As discussed before, the objective when optimizing financial dynamics is to optimize cash flow. If there is no cash flow impact, the change proposed adds little or no financial value to the organization.[4] The difficult component is modeling the financial dynamics to ensure that the equations represent cash in a way that is directly reflected on the financial statements. The same holds true for the constraints. Constraints must be modeled, too, to ensure that its dynamics are represented in a way that closely resembles the impact on the financial dynamics represented by the organization's financial statements.

There are four types of problems being considered, and they are based on the components of cash flow dynamics. This section will seek to optimize cash flow by discussing how to:

- Optimize revenues (maximize)
- Optimize costs (minimize)
- Optimize margins/profits (maximize)
- Optimize working capital (minimize)

The rest of this section will discuss the optimization of each and will also discuss ways to improve each, even if the solution is not an optimal solution.

Maximizing Revenues

Maximizing the revenues of a process can be done most directly by focusing on maximum throughput. Other ways to organizationally improve revenues, such as redesigning processes to add value that can increase price or by considering process designs that ultimately increase the market reach, are beyond the scope of this section. This section, along with those that follow, will assume that the objective is to optimize the current state rather than to consider the redesign of the processes.

Objective

To maximize revenues, one must maximize the amount of revenue brought into the organization through the process. The most obvious ways to do this simply are to maximize throughput and price of products that are sold. Increasing throughput of products that are not yet sold may not increase revenues. They increase inventory, lead time, and potentially customer service, but revenues may or may not increase. One must ensure that the inventory of finished goods is, in fact, ultimately sold to model the process effectively and, therefore, receive the benefits of optimizing throughputs. Otherwise, producing that which is unnecessary takes up time and capital and does not produce revenues. Additionally, if the inventory becomes obsolete, its value might significantly hurt the organization financially.

Revenue models for processes must, therefore, go a step beyond that required for model throughput. The model must consider products not only produced but sold, too. Otherwise, the model will provide financial information, such as unrealistic revenue projections, that does not represent the reality of the situation being modeled.

Influencing Factors

Maximizing revenues requires a number of issues to be considered:

- Knowledge of demand
- A model for revenue dynamics
- Policies that seek to minimize production of items that are not sold
- Potential reduction of lead time

EXHIBIT 7.13

Three products with their individual prices.

Product	Price
A	$10
B	$20
C	$30

Knowledge of Demand

Knowledge of demand is critical because it is demand that should dictate the output and throughput of the process. Once the demand-based throughput is determined, capacity and operating rules for the operations that make up the processes should be determined. To the greatest extent possible, process output should align to sold demand, but this is not always possible. In highly seasonal products, one may have to spend the entire off-season producing what is anticipated at the peak sales periods, which can be 11 months away in some cases.

A Model for Revenue Dynamics

A model for revenue dynamics will be tough to create when modeling for forecasted demand. Organizations must be willing to look at the past forecasted demand and actual demand and determine how to reconcile the differences in the model. Another component when considering maximizing the throughput of multiple items is not only the price but the rate of generating revenues. Consider, for example, three products for which there is demand (see Exhibit 7.13).

If you were to maximize revenues with this information, you may choose to produce as much of product C as possible. However, when considering the information contained in Exhibit 7.14, you may change your answers. When looking at Exhibit 7.15, however, all should completely change their point of view.

EXHIBIT 7.14

Three products with their processing times at two operations.

Product	Operation 1 processing time	Operation 2 processing time
A	10 minutes	15 minutes
B	12 minutes	35 minutes
C	30 minutes	50 minutes

EXHIBIT 7.15

Three products with their price and revenue generation rate.

Product	Price	Revenue Generation (rate/hour)
A	$10	$40.00
B	$20	$32.26
C	$30	$36.00

Notice that the revenue generation rate is impacted by the processing time on constraint.

When operation time is factored into the model, a new component of the problem is introduced. Throughput and revenue generation rate must both be considered. Product A generates greater revenues because of the fact that Operation 2, the constraint, can make the product at a faster rate than it can make products B and C. The speed at which product A is created makes up for the difference in price. So, while there may be high-priced items available for production, price is not the only factor to be considered when determining whether to make a product. The rate at which revenues can be generated at this price, given production constraints, becomes important.

Policies that Minimize Overproduction

As mentioned earlier, production well in anticipation of demand is unavoidable in some cases. In many cases, however, it is just an excuse to keep machines and people working. While this may be a good cause, it impacts the operational and financial performance of the organization negatively. From an operational performance perspective, working for the sake of working requires items on which the operation can process. This means excess inventory, and excess inventory increases lead times. If the organization is producing products that have not been sold and an order comes in, the order must either wait until products that have not been sold are finished processing or it must disrupt the production and order of the items currently being processed. These disruptions impact the utilization of the operations, and it may require extra capacity to manage the process. In this situation, organizations are not only negatively impacting revenues, they require higher cost structure, as well.

Organizations do better when they are fast enough, flexible enough, and confident enough to produce less of what is not necessary and more of what is necessary. If the organization must continue to produce products for which there is no demand, it is likely that the organization is carrying too much capacity and may want to consider permanently reducing capacity or creating flexible capacity through the creation of a temporary workforce. Additionally, this overproduction may hide problems of overcapacity leading to perpetually suboptimized operations.

Reducing Lead Time

Reducing overall lead time does not necessarily have a direct impact on creating revenues. If the maximum throughput is 10 parts per hour, regardless of whether the queue is 1 minute or 5, the output is the same. The revenue generation rate takes this into consideration when its analysis is performed. Lead time may impact customer satisfaction. A process with a long queue may create discontent with the market, which may have a negative long-term effect on revenues.

Optimizing Costs

Objective

To optimize costs, one seeks the minimum cost level obtainable. The minimum cost level should be subject to output constraints. For example, minimize costs subject to the need to produce 10,000 of product A and 5,000 of product B. In a case such as this one, the objective is to figure out what the lowest-cost solution would be to achieve a certain output goal. Without an expected output or activity level, the lowest cost solution is to eliminate the need for the product altogether (including considering outsourcing for which the organization may still pay), not perform the activity at all, and eliminate the capacity. However, this is often not feasible, so operations must seek other solutions.

The need to constrain costs is very similar to minimizing the amount of input capacity necessary to allow the process to function but takes the concept a step or two further. Input can be minimized without minimizing the costs that impact the cash flow. One can reassign capacity from one process to another and the bottom line will not see a cost impact. So, whereas a cost center may see a profit for such actions, the bottom line and, therefore, the cash flow remain the same. Cash flow–based models must, therefore, reflect the costs and decisions that increase or decrease bottom-line costs. Otherwise, managers and analysts are fooling themselves into believing that their optimization models will increase profitability and cash flow.

Cost-Based Cash Flow Models to Represent Influencing Factors

One cost dynamics model that works very well with cost optimization models is explicit cost dynamics. Explicit cost dynamics is a cost management, versus cost accounting, tool, and the basis for the development of the concept was bottom-line cost dynamics. The emphasis of the approach is to identify resources, actions, and items, to understand their cost dynamics and how they cause costs to be incurred, and to provide methods and cost models to help effectively model and manage costs. With explicit cost dynamics, the process and operation can be modeled using the cost models and can seek the minimum cost level necessary to achieve the desired output level. Since the costs are tied directly to the bottom line, integrity is maintained between the cost model and the bottom line and cash flow.

An economics-based cost model can be considered, as well. This should be considered in lieu of an accounting-based cost model. Economics-based cost models tend to emphasize how costs are incurred by the organization and are much more closely aligned with the true cost dynamics than accounting-based costs. Accounting-based costs, whether financial accounting-based or managerial accounting-based (standard costing and activity-based costing, alike), should seldom, if at all, be the basis for optimization that seeks cost minimization from a cash flow perspective. Due to the flawed math associated with allocating costs, the model can create cost dynamics that are contrary to what the bottom line will see. If the bottom line is reflected incorrectly, the cash flow, too, will be incorrectly modeled.

Consider the following as a simple proof. How can costs go down as one does more? At least the same amount of capacity must be utilized to do more, and unless labor is paid less for doing more, for instance, the cost at least remains the same. As more activities are performed, one incurs increased action costs. The net result is that costs remain the same or go up, not down, as one does more. As long as accounting has this flaw, it will be very difficult to use costs generated by the accounting system as input for an optimization model.

Another decision that an effectively defined cost optimization model can aid in making is make-versus-buy analyses. For a given output level, the cost dynamics can be modeled to determine whether it is cheaper to maintain the process or to outsource it. Again, the right model is necessary. The math and limiting assumptions of an accounting-based model will limit the effectiveness of the solutions. For example, in an accounting-based model where costs are allocated to a unit, one determines a cost of that unit: say, five cents. If the same unit can be purchased for three cents from the outside, accounting models would typically recommend buying the product from the outside. Accounting models typically do not suggest or take the requisite next steps of identifying the fact that the capacity still exists in many cases. The net result is a cost increase, not a cost decrease. Explicit cost dynamics has techniques to manage the situation effectively. As products are purchased from the outside, the model shows a cost increase and provides the data necessary to figure out what costs must be eliminated to achieve the desired or optimal cost level.

Optimizing Profit

Optimizing profit is often a more desirable model than optimizing revenues alone or optimizing costs alone. Optimizing revenues independently of costs can lead to increased revenues but may increase costs, as well, which, depending on the situation, can either increase profit, keep it the same, or reduce it, based on the rate of increase of revenues and of costs. Modeling costs alone can limit the ability to generate revenues, again, potentially impacting profitability in a negative way.

 TIPS & TECHNIQUES

To the greatest extent possible, you should seek to optimize profits rather than revenues or costs individually. Profit has trade-off management built in. Optimizing revenues can increase costs, and optimizing costs can reduce revenues.

Objective

When optimizing profits, one seeks the maximum profit possible. The objective, therefore, is to maximize the difference between revenues and costs. It is recommended that the model be bottom-line profit-based rather than unit profit-based, because the assumptions necessary to create an effective unit-based model, where one seeks unit margins, are not in line with the bottom-line cost dynamics.

Within the model, therefore, the objective is a level of throughput and input that creates the best output for the organization, given its constraints. The constraints may be capacity-related, meaning that there may be a minimum required level of capacity (e.g., organizations that do not lay off people) or a maximum level of capacity (labor is available for 16 hours or less). The revenue component may emphasize the fact that at least X of one product or at most Y of another product must be created. The objective and the constraints all go into the model and, when solved, desired output, throughput, and input levels are determined.

There are a number of ways to model such situations, and doing so in detail is really beyond the scope of this book. The purpose of this section is simply to recommend that when seeking to optimize financial dynamics, optimizing profitability should strongly be considered. Optimizing revenues can aid growth and sometimes market share, but not necessarily profit. Minimizing costs can be important for organizations that are in declining or stagnant models, and organizations should always seek capacity levels that are the least cost. However, cost optimization can often reduce capacity in a way that harms throughput, such as eliminating important revenue-generating capacity. Organizations should, therefore, seek the optimal profit level to ensure desired results. If there are demand constraints (throughput is less than or equal to W), that situation can be reflected in a profit model, just as it can in a cost model. However, by incorporating revenues in the overall model, the math and, therefore, the managers have more solution degrees of freedom, which are likely to lead to a more global solution.

Optimizing Working Capital

Objective

Optimizing working capital involves solving the objective in Equation 7.4. Inventory-purchased does not become operating revenue until sold. Receivables really do not mean much until collected. This combination can represent a major component of an organization's cash that it does not have and is, therefore, not a desirable situation from a cash flow perspective. Payables reflect the money that an organization owes others, the longer it can have cash working to increase nonoperating income through investments.

$$\begin{matrix} \text{minimize working} = \text{working inventory} + \text{accounts receivable} \\ \text{capital} \qquad - \text{accounts payable} \end{matrix} \qquad 7.4$$

Modeling working capital is a fairly complicated task, however. The constraints will often have strategic and operational components. From a strategic perspective, one may want to reduce receivables by collecting its money more quickly. Solutions such as rapid and effective billing and collections can aid, as can strongly enforced and aggressive payment schedules and penalties in reducing cash that has not been collected. With payables, organizations must consider ways to extend their payment as long as the organization to which the payment is being made allows. Organizations in a highly effective operating supply chain may want to strongly consider the impact of such actions. Those who try to extend payment beyond reasonable time limits and expect relatively immediate payment on their end may find themselves being less-than-ideal citizens by vendors and customers within the chain. A firm will not want the practices to have a negative impact on the performance of the supply chain. Additionally, such actions can impact the organization's financial value, which might limit its ability to be as effective as it might be with a better cash flow situation. Regardless, the rules for payment and receipt, based on the organization's strategy, must, therefore, be modeled into the constraints.

From an operational level, the working-capital model should integrate into a financial or operational model. Inventory, for example, must be tied to a profit, revenue, or throughput model. Determining inventory in the absence of demand and operations expectations will likely yield solutions that have inventory levels that are either too large or too small. The true value has no context and, therefore, little use. Therefore, the inventory must be constrained by expected production rates and by the minimum and maximum inventory levels determined by inventory management.

Summary

The purpose of this chapter was to introduce the reader to the concept of optimization. Optimization is a very powerful tool that can be used to seek optimal solutions. It can also be used, as often discussed throughout the chapter, as a benchmark for operational or financial objectives. Finally, optimization models and their solutions can provide guidelines or ideas for ways to improve the operations within an organization. Concepts such as revenue generation rate, which could also be expanded to profit generation rate, are generally applicable whether working in an optimal environment.

The next chapter will take all the ideas that have been discussed to this point and combine them, with the other concepts, into a four-step model for managing capacity.

Endnotes

[1] Throughput $= \dfrac{d\,(output)}{dt}$. This simply means that throughput measures the rate of change of output over time. Another measure that is important to consider for variance analysis and root cause analysis is the second derivative of output $= \dfrac{d^2\,(output)}{dt^2}$. This ratio represents the rate of change of throughput. If the derivative is positive, throughput is increasing. If negative, throughput is decreasing. Considering output, the second derivative describes whether the rate of output is increasing or decreasing. So, although the throughput may be increasing (positive first derivative of output), it may be increasing at a slower rate (negative second derivative of output), which may be important information when planning capacity or when the process cannot meet demand.

[2] Assume that operations are acting at their desired levels.

[3] See for example, Joseph G. Monk's *Schaum's Outlines of Theory and Problems of Operations Management,* Schaum's Outline Series (New York: McGraw-Hill, Inc., 1985).

[4] Assuming that cash flow based analyses are the only determinant of market value. There are other components of valuing an organization such as management competence and others which solutions might be able to impact.

CHAPTER 8

Elements of Effective Capacity Management

After reading this chapter, you will be able to:

- Describe the four steps to effective capacity management
- Discuss the basics of demand planning and the impact on capacity
- Understand how to align capacity with demand
- Understand the importance of defining and implementing proper measures
- Define continuous improvement and the role that it plays when managing capacity

Introduction

To this point in the book, we have discussed all of the elements of capacity management. We began with the fundamental components of capacity. We assembled them into operations. The operations were assembled into processes. We then discussed the financial dynamics of operations and processes. In the last chapter, we discussed optimization and how to optimize processes. This chapter will emphasize a four-step model to help organizations effectively manage capacity.

Four Steps to Effective Capacity Management

Capacity management is a topic that is often simple to comprehend but difficult to practice. The simplicity comes from the fact that when one is armed with the right information in the absence of policy and procedure-related constraints, determining how to manage capacity is fairly simple. However, gaining the right information and the policy- and procedure-related constraints are what create the complexity component of managing capacity.

The tools and techniques used to this point should aid the manager in understanding how to obtain and use the information required to manage capacity. The previous chapters also provide guidance for setting policies and procedures at a high level in some cases, but to do so effectively will require organizations to look within their culture, their market, and their competencies to find their unique stand on policies and procedures.

This chapter provides a four-step model for managing capacity regardless of the organization's existing operational environment. The four steps for effective capacity management are:

- Demand planning
- Capacity alignment
- Effective measurement
- Continuous improvement

This four-step model is a closed-loop system that can be applied to practically any organization regardless of policy and procedure issues. Clearly, the presence of such issues will constrain the ability to manage capacity. Those responsible for decision-making will have to decide whether this priority approach makes sense for the organization.

Define the Model

The model proposed here represents ideas about capacity and continuous improvement that have been in existence for a long period of time.

The model begins with the concept of a forecast. The forecast is important because it is the forecasted demand for the product created by the process that dictates the output level of the process. Whether manufacturing components or cutting invoices, anticipated demand is the first place to begin to determine capacity.

The next step is to align capacity with the anticipated demand. Such techniques have been in existence almost as long as capacity planning has been in existence. Techniques such as rough-cut capacity planning, detailed capacity planning, resource requirements planning, and other techniques have allowed organizations to plan their capacity levels for the anticipated demand. In our case, the objective is to align with the demand not only from an operational perspective but to use the optimization tools to help determine how to align financially with the demand, as well. Just because there is demand does not mean that the organization must expend all of its resources in an attempt to meet the demand. The alignment will be used to set throughput and lead time expectations for the process.

With this information known, the organization must determine how it will measure the process on a more tactical level. These measures will, in turn, be used to dictate the capacity levels of the operations. The operations will then operate to meet the objectives set forth by the process. This process will ensure integrity between the optimization model and the measures used to support processes. Finally, the organization must take its information and feed it back into the process to improve in subsequent rounds.

Demand Planning

To manage capacity effectively, you must understand something about the particular workload that will exist and must be positioned to meet capacity requirements over a period of time. The anticipated work and the type of work will dictate what the process must be able to accomplish during that time. It will be the process expectations that determine the amount and types of capacity required.

Forecasting is an activity that seeks to predict future demand. Since it is a guess, it is usually, but not always, wrong. Many factors that are controlled by the forecaster can influence the accuracy of a forecast. One of the influencing factors is the time horizon. Another factor is the forecasting technique used. Another is the data-gathering method used, and the final factor considered here is whether the process allows for closing the loop by feeding in previous information and error rates to improve the process.

Time Horizon

The time horizon has much to do with the accuracy of a forecast. The longer the forecast horizon, the less likely that the forecast will be correct. The weatherperson, for example, can predict the weather tomorrow fairly accurately but will struggle achieving the same accuracy for the same date next year. There are too many factors and too much unknown information that can surface between when the forecast is made and when the demand is realized. So, to increase forecast accuracy, you should work to make the time horizon as short as possible. There is a potential problem with this technique, however. Organizations may not have time to adjust their capacity if they can only operate from short time horizons, so you must take into account the flexibility and elasticity of your operations and capacity, respectively. Another way to improve forecast accuracies is to eliminate, to the greatest extent possible, any uncertainty that may exist.

Organizations with relatively steady demand and predictable demand patterns can be relatively sure that after seeking optimal capacity levels based on this demand, major changes to capacity levels, once they reach the time within which one can fairly accurately predict demand, do not occur. So, long- or short-term forecasts will not have a major impact on its capacity. What about organizations with varying demand levels and patterns? Long-term, incorrect forecasts might cause the organization to guess capacity levels incorrectly. Additionally, the organization may find adjusting capacity upward and downward to be difficult. Short-term, more correct forecasts are nice to have in their situation, but getting the information this late does not help the organization much if at all. They must, therefore, try to improve their ability to predict demand for longer planning horizons to the greatest extent possible.

Such an organizational environment also has two other options: taking an operational position or taking a financial position. Operationally, as we talk about alignment in the next section, the organization can have permanent capacity and temporary capacity to make up the differences between what was forecasted and the resulting actual demand. From a financial perspective, important decisions must be made. Should the organization seek to maximize revenues by assuming, optimistically, that the higher end of the forecasting distribution is most likely to be correct? The result will be the capacity to ensure that all revenues that are possible to be received by this firm are, in fact, received. The conservative approach may be more pessimistic about the forecast and may choose a capacity-limiting strategy, which seeks to optimize revenues or profits subject to the constraint that capacity remains the same.

Technique

There are a number of forecasting techniques that exist, from complete guesses to "increase last year's forecast by 3%" to "our distributors told us that their customers would buy X" to very sophisticated models that attempt to identify and pick up trends in demand and make predictions based on the trends. In different situations, each has its own merits. Unfortunately, experience has shown that organizations often do not use the right techniques in the right situations.

The level of detail and the extent to which an organization seeks an accurate forecast depend on what people do with the information. A very sophisticated model is no more useful than a spreadsheet if the organization is not going to act on the information. In some organizations, much time and money have been spent doing market and sales analysis and building a forecast based on observed trends, only to have the forecast dismissed by production as marketing propaganda. Production then determines its own forecasts. In another situation, production looked at the forecast at a very detailed level performing their capacity and materials planning from this data. What they did not know, however, was that the data were from distributors who, with no forecasting sophistication, guessed what their customers would buy. Sales then adjusted the numbers upward by a large, arbitrary amount.

Technique often determines the degree to which a forecast is wrong, all things being equal. The questions, when determining forecasting technique and investing in the tools to perform forecasting, are: what is the magnitude of the variance, what is the cause of the variance, and what is the value of this variance? If a technique has been significantly incorrect in the past, the magnitude may be significantly off. Additionally, certain activities, which happen during the cycle being planned and without the knowledge of the demand planners, can create differences, as well. If the forecast is regularly incorrect to a great extent, the organization may want to switch forecasting techniques. When considering the variance, what is the cause of the variance, one should ask about how the organization will be impacted by the variance from a financial perspective, operational perspective, and from a customer service perspective. Financially and operationally, the revenues or costs might be incorrect because decisions were made based on erroneous data, leading to losses. From a customer service perspective, not having what is desired when it is desired is an experience that few of us like to experience from either side of the fence. When deciding on a forecasting process, one must understand what data will be necessary, who will use them, how will they use them—thus establishing a process for forecasting as defined in Chapters 4 and 5.

Data Gathering and Cleansing

Even the best forecasting technique is useless without good data. Poor data yield poor forecasts and create a poor foundation for capacity planning and management. Hence, given the type of forecast and how the data are used, those responsible for the forecast must also be ultimately responsible for ensuring that the data are properly gathered. This means providing the expectations, parameters, and sometimes the tools, so forecasting can occur more effectively. If the distributor is guessing, on what premises are they making guesses? Are there tools or techniques that can be introduced to the distributors that could help them formalize their forecasts? Are there past forecasts and actual demand data for the same periods that can be used to determine error rates? With such an error rate and with some smoothing techniques, one can begin to reduce the amount of forecast error. In the absence of specific information, you may seek to limit the unknown and quantify it so that risk is reduced to only that which is completely unknown.[1]

Cleansing forecast input data, and even some output data, is often a tough process. It is tough not because the process itself is challenging but because it can become highly political. Some organizations roll up the forecasts generated by their sales personnel to a vice president of sales. The vice president looks at an aggregate forecast and decides that it is either too high or too low and often, without enough data to accurately make the call, changes the forecast. The forecast may then need to be approved by yet another person or committee who may make their own adjustments. By the time the forecast is approved for planning purposes, it bears little resemblance to how it started.

Situations such as this one suggest a culture and measures that are incorrect and must be replaced not for the purpose of capacity management alone but in the name of building a great company. From a capacity management perspective, since the forecast sets the stage for throughput levels and, therefore, capacity levels, as the numbers change to reflect personal agendas, these decisions could result in allocating resources that result in losses for the firm. Such decisions can lead to carrying too much capacity when there is no demand to support it or not enough capacity when the demand exists.

Closing the Loop

Forecasted demand data and actual demand data are both very useful information to have when making a new forecast. There was likely a process used to generate previous forecasts, regardless of how crude or sophisticated the forecasting technique. Comparing actual demand to forecasted demand will create opportunities to understand the strengths and weaknesses of the process used to forecast. The information can also be used as a way to adjust future forecasts by taking the variance into account.

The variance between the forecasted demand and the actual demand represents the difference between the forecast and reality. The objective over time is to improve the forecasting model and the ability of the organization to improve its forecasts. Having a repeatable forecasting process is the first step. Regardless of how crude the process may or may not be, it needs to be stable and predictable. This allows for an understanding of the components and assumptions that went into the forecast. Once known and documented, the analysis can begin to compare the assumptions that went into the model and the respective reality. Adjustments can often be made that lead to an improved forecasting model. This process of analyzing and continually reducing variance should be viewed as a positive activity. Penalties should result from changing forecast results to reflect a personal agenda but not from using the process and getting a forecast with a large variance. If the process is forever incorrect, one may look to develop a better process or tool but at least the process for creating the variance is relatively standard and predictable. The objective is to seek continuous improvement, so that the forecast model ultimately reflects reality as closely as it can.

IN THE REAL WORLD

Improving Your Forecasting and Forecast Response

In their article *Rocket Science Retailing Is Almost Here: Are You Ready?* the authors address some fundamental concerns about how organizations forecast and offer some techniques for improving forecasting techniques.[a]

- Update forecasts based on early sales data. Often, variability between forecasted demand and actual demand can be very useful for predicting actual demand for the entire period.

- Track and predict forecast accuracy. Knowing how, why, and to what extent the forecast is incorrect can be a source of much information, such as how to interpret forecasted demand either from a supplier or from a system that generates the forecast.

- Get the product-testing right. How, when, and where one tries to determine future demand is critical for determining how correct the projected demand will be.

- Use a wide variety of forecasting approaches. With many forecasting techniques, an organization can look at the assumptions in each model to help improve overall forecasting.

[a] Marshall L. Fisher, Ananth Raman, and Anna Sheen McClelland, "Rocket Science Retailing Is Almost Here: Are You Ready?" *Harvard Business Review* 78, 4 (July–August 2000).

Capacity Alignment

Capacity alignment is the process of determining what capacity levels should exist, given the operational and financial expectations placed on the process. Simply, it is the process that converts demand to capacity via the process. This step is a very important one because without it, there is nothing concrete to which the capacity can be aligned. Without this information, how can one optimize the processes for financial objectives, operational objectives, or both?

The approach recommended for capacity alignment is to view the demand and determine whether the current process can achieve the demand levels. If the demand can be met, the next steps involve determining the desired product sequences and mixes and then determining the right measurement levels for the operations within the process. If the organization cannot meet the demand, there are options. The first option is to limit capacity to the currently available capacity and seek to optimize output based on this value. One can also seek to gain capacity by either increasing internal capacity or by seeking external capacity. In either case, the organization must make decisions that will align the capacity with the demand.

Meeting the Output

If the organization can meet the anticipated output, it means that there is excess capacity and that the constraint is the market. When this is the case, a couple of strategic decisions must be made. First, if it is anticipated that this is going to be a long-term issue, the organization might want to consider reducing its capacity. Another option would be to consider seeking additional demand for the capacity. There are numerous ways that this can be done, such as outsourcing the capacity, moving the capacity into other areas of the business for which there is demand, or, given the competence of the capacity, spin it off. Excessive low-utilized capacity is not something that an organization will want on its books for extensive periods of time.

From a short-term perspective, those managing the process have a couple of responsibilities. As they schedule the operations, they may want to still consider the proper sequencing of orders to minimize processing time. This does two things. First, it supports maintaining high customer satisfaction levels. Just because there is not enough demand does not mean that an organization should extend lead times beyond what they could be unless there were some sort of strategic reason for doing so. Second, if minimizing total processing time frees up the capacity to do other work, additional revenues may be realized. Finally, efficient operations create a realistic picture of excess capacity. This, in turn, can lead to effective capacity reduction.

Once the schedule sequence has been determined, the measures can be put in place. Availability and utilization can be measured. The recommended approach is to always focus on high utilization and adjust the availability of the operation. For example, an operation can be available for 16 hours per day and utilized at 50% for 8 hours, or the operation can be available for 8 hours per day and utilized at 100% for all 8 hours. In the former, the organization may have to pay for excess capacity that is only partially being used. They may, depending on the situation, be able to reduce a shift and still produce what is necessary. The trade-off is that the planners may require that the operation produce in larger batches. While this may save paying for excess capacity, it may also may increase lead time. In such situations, you may want to consider developing an optimization model to determine the optimal solution.

Demand Exceeds Capacity

When demand exceeds capacity, the capacity becomes the constraint. Specifically, the process is a constraint, and those managing the process must figure out how to get the most from the process. There are three options for the organization in this case. The first option is to choose to maximize profits, throughput, or revenues subject to the constraints that exist. In other words, keep the process as it is and figure out what products to make, given the constraints. The second option is to consider increasing the relative capacity by outsourcing work to another organization. The third option would be to increase the capacity of the current process by supplementing the capacity that exists with other capacity entities or operations owned by the organization.

Optimizing Current State

Chapter 7 focused on optimizing, so that discussion will not be repeated here. The important point here is ensuring that it is the availability of the equipment that is adjusted when the measures are defined. The nonconstraint resources have excess capacity, by definition. Therefore, to keep them from carrying too much capacity, the availability should be reduced to the point where the throughput targets can still be maintained.

Outsourcing

Outsourcing involves finding capacity that exists elsewhere and using it for the purposes of meeting demand or for attempting to lower the cost of production. In this case, the objective is to find out how more revenues can be generated by increasing capacity. Outsourcing may be a good temporary situation because you pay a transaction cost for the units that you receive from the outsourcing organization. The transaction is clear and the benefits are clear. Gaining extra capacity will allow the organization to achieve additional revenues, but you must factor increased revenues bringing along with them the cost of goods sold from a financial accounting perspective, meaning that increasing revenues does not go directly to the bottom line. The costs may even increase because of the premium that may be charged by the outsourcing client, depending on the services provided. Such a situation should involve a decent financial analysis to determine whether it is a sound decision. Organizations doing this without being careful may find themselves destroying economic value.

Adding Capacity

Adding capacity at the constraints can always be a consideration. This can happen by working overtime or by hiring additional employees, buying more equipment, or by adding on other capacity entities or operations. Managers should be able to explicitly define what improvements in throughput are going to be achieved by increasing costs by bringing in more capacity.

Regardless of the approach taken to align with the expected demand, the measurements will all be the same. Managers will want to identify the measures that give them an understanding of the capacity levels involved in a process, the operational performance of the process, and the financial performance of the process. The next section focuses on ensuring effective measurements.

Effective Measurement

The previous two sections discussed the importance of forecasting and aligning with the forecast. The purpose is to align the capacity with the work that is expected of it. The next step involves ensuring that the alignment occurred effectively and identifying opportunity areas that are targets for improvements in the future. An effective measurement system provides answers to important questions. You may want to know how much capacity exists at any given moment. You may want to understand the competence of this capacity. You may want to know the forecast accuracy. You may want to know whether an investment in additional capacity provides an improvement on the bottom line, cash flow, and the organization's economic value.

There are a large number of ways to measure performance, and many are situation specific. This section, therefore, will address key points to help ensure that the measurement system provides the right information from the perspectives of demand, capacity, operations, and financials.

Capacity

An organization must know how much capacity it has and how effectively it is operating. From knowing how much capacity an organization has, it can determine the cost of the capacity. By knowing how effectively the capacity is operating, decisions can be made to determine whether to expand and where expansion should occur. Basic capacity measures were discussed in Chapters 3 and 6. To reiterate some of the basics, measuring capacity involves combining the basic entities and capacity measures into operations with certain capabilities. Sometimes the capacity is known, such as when looking at the operating rate of a machine, and sometimes it is determined through experimentation. Regardless, it is important to always have an understanding of how much capacity is in the organization.

Another criterion to consider is whether and how the capacity is being utilized. Managers will want to understand the availability of the capacity to ensure that they are getting what they are paying for. Utilization, too, is important but perhaps not as important as availability. Availability provides flexibility. You may not want the capacity to operate all of the time, depending on the demand being placed on it (utilization), but you will want to be able to operate the capacity when it is desirable to do so (availability). Finally, you will want to understand on what the capacity spends its time. This will help the organization understand the capacity demands created by certain processes. Processes that demand significant capacity must either generate generous financial returns for the organization or must be very important strategically. Otherwise, it may ultimately require the organization to maintain capacity for which the returns are small, which is clearly a less-than-desirable situation.

Operations

As described previously in Chapters 5 and 7, the key measures for operational performance are throughput and lead time. These measures will dictate the levels of availability and utilization necessary to meet demand. Sometimes, especially when seeking to optimize a process from a revenue or profit perspective, throughput, as it relates to sales, can be quite important. The products made and not sold do not contribute to improvements in revenues and, therefore, cannot be counted in the model.

Financials

There are multiple measures that you will want to consider from a financial perspective. There are the traditional measures introduced in Chapter 6 that emphasized revenues, costs, and working capital. Those will not be repeated here. Other measures that you may want to consider, however, are financial losses and gains from decisions made to increase or decrease capacity.

When comparing demand to capacity, the difference between the two can be considered a loss of some sort. If, for instance, capacity is lower than demand, the unfulfilled demand can be considered a loss of revenues. If the capacity is greater than demand, the loss is one of having excessive costs. Given the existence of demand and capacity data, such measures can be very important in helping organizations determine how effectively they are managing capacity not only to ensure profitability but to improve capacity management, also.

Continuous Improvement

Continuous improvement emphasizes time and the desire to always seek improvement over time. There are a number of ways to do so. First, there must be a culture that always seeks a better solution. The current state is never good enough. There are always opportunities to improve. Second, the people in the organization must have tools, techniques, and measurements that will help them seek and test for a better solution. Third, the improvements must be fed back into the system and the improved performance measured and documented. Finally, many organizations will reward the people who come up with improvements to the system, however large or small. Such programs will consider even non–value-adding solutions to be worthy of a prize because the worker took time to think about an improvement and suggested the improvement. They are rewarding the process, in this case. By not rewarding the workers, the message being sent is that only certain suggestions are worthy of rewards. Organizations may not want to send these messages to its employees because they do not want to people to stop seeking improvements in the working environment.

As with many other sections in this book, the concept here is not new.[2] The suggestion is that the organization should take an existing approach and apply it to capacity management to ensure long-term growth and improvement. There are a few important components of continuous improvement that should be introduced because they tend to be very successful:

- Variance analysis
- Cause analysis
- Defining improvements
- Feedback

Variance Analysis

Variance analysis involves measuring an achieved value and comparing it to what was expected. The difference is a variance. So, actual throughput can be compared to planned throughput, actual utilization to planned utilization. Once the difference is identified, you can use tools, such as cause analysis, to determine the causes for the variations. The important issue is to ensure that the right data exist and that managers are going after the right problems. Oftentimes, organizations perform variance analysis of the data that they have collected rather than on the data that provide the desired information. This is similar to the cliché where one looks under a light for the keys that they have lost in the dark. It is convenient to look under the light, although the keys are not there.

Cause Analysis

Cause analyses are very common techniques that are used to identify causes of an undesirable situation. Simply, you define the problem and begin performing an analysis on the problem to find the potential causes of the problem. In this case, a cause analysis can be performed on the

 TIPS & TECHNIQUES

The variance and cause analyses are critical to managing capacity. The analyses must provide the extent of the loss and the causes of the loss. As the process is understood, it can be improved and become more flexible. It will even have an increased ability to respond to changes in demand. This increased flexibility affords the ability to manage capacity to demand a bit more closely. This will give the organization many more options in terms of managing its capacity to varying demand.

results from the variance analysis. The potential causes for a variance that may exist between actual availability and planned availability can be analyzed. With many analytic approaches, it begins by identifying potential causes for the variance and then searches for the reasons of the causes and creates a diagram of potential causes for the variance. Other approaches start with influences on availability and seeks to understand which of the influencing factors created this particular variance. Regardless of the technique, the objectives are the same: to find out why variances exist and to eliminate the cause.

Defining Improvements

Once the cause of the variance is defined, the next step is to identify improvements. This is often a fairly straightforward process once an effective cause analysis has been created. The difficulty often does not involve creating the solution. The difficulty is often incurred when implementing the solution or *attempting* to do so. Many times, cause analyses point to limitations or constraints created by policies, procedures, or politics. Organizations that seek to continuously improve must create an environment where the objective is improvement, rather than managing personal agendas.

Feedback

All information gained in this process should be fed back into the process. In this way, future iterations of identifying demand, aligning with the demand, and measuring the results will benefit from the knowledge gained each time through the process. Capacity management should be viewed as an ongoing journey of continuously improving. One will never forecast well enough. One will never perfectly align capacity with demand to create no losses. Measures are often difficult to come by or to collect. As long as these imperfections exist, there will be opportunities to improve how you manage your capacity.

Summary

Capacity management should be a process of continuous improvement. Due the the nature of the variables used to make capacity designs, there will always be ways to improve your operations. The first step will be to look at capacity management as a closed-loop process. Input the decision, operational, and financial data into the process, let the system process the data, and review the output. Once the output is reviewed, updates can be made to the input variables to improve to process even more. Looking at capacity in this manner will ensure continual improvement of both operations and finances. Not looking at it in this manner, however, creates opportunities where "lessons learned" could be lost forever. Additionally, increased organizational competence resulting from improving and refining processes will not occur. It will be difficult to obtain and sustain a competitive advantage without these fundamental competencies.

Endnotes

1 Hugh Courtney, *20-20 Foresight: Crafting Strategy in an Uncertain World* (Cambridge, MA: Harvard Business School Press, 2001).

2 Masaaki Imai, *Kaizen: The Key to Japan's Competitive Success* (New York: McGraw-Hill, Inc., 1986).

Index